The RIGHT is WRONG!

Never underestimate the power of stupid people in large groups

The Bullet Theory

Dr. Jay Polmar

Table of Contents

Preface

I'm an old man, almost 70, watching the world deteriorate before my very eyes from trusting governments to negotiate with terrorists for a peaceful world. It's insanity. It's not only the terrorism organizations of the world, Boko Harum, ISIS, Al-Qaeda, etc. This includes our own police departments. Yes, our own police are terrorizing and killing innocent men, women, and children. Or, maybe they are not that innocent. But, choking a man to death for supposedly selling single cigarettes in Staten Island, (which taxes were paid on when he bought then), and then discovering, after they killed him, that he didn't have a single cigarette on him, is a violation of the law. Legal (tax paid) or illegal (without tax paid) what's the difference, the police murdered an innocent man by choking him to death without any evidence of his wrong-doing.

Or, another young man who supposedly had an illegal knife in Baltimore, but the knife wasn't illegal, and they broke his back while arresting him. And, rather than taking him to the hospital – they drove him around in a police van, and he died on arrival to the police station – or within an hour later. You'll never get to the truth with cops like that.

Or, how about the killing of a young boy for playing with a toy gun, or wrestling a young girl who was at a pool party and forcing her to the ground because she didn't have a pool pass – except she did have the pool pass. Or, the police in South Carolina pulling a 16 year old girl from her high school class desk-chair and throwing her half-way across the floor, and the Republicans said the policeman acted within the law, and videos showed his brutality, all because she looked at her iPhone. And I can go on and on about how the police have no respect for anyone – and act like terrorists within a terrorist organization – but why the fuck bother. Yes, why the fuck bother – no one does anything to stop this abuse.

And I am watching the terrorists of the Republican Party threaten an end to Medicare, Food Stamps, Medicaid, Obamacare (which was originally a Republican idea), Educational Funding, Social Security, and must I go on. The foundation of America is rotten to the core already but is rotting away further and very quickly, through the US Congress, which is made up of millionaires, most who got their millions from political corruption and payoffs.

The US has one of the worst educational systems in the Free World, somewhere around 23rd in a recent quality assessment. Healthcare is down there also – terrible healthcare, and I am a crippled victim of what the US healthcare system can do; yes, American doctors crippled me! Cuba's healthcare is far better – and FREE even for visitors, just like Mexico!

But what I am getting at, overall, is the US system has deteriorated and made billionaires out of low-life Republicans who illegally waged war, in Iraq. Why do I say illegally? Because there never were Weapons of Mass Destruction, it was a ruse to engage Iraq and Saddam Hussein in war, when the culprits were really Iran, Saudi Arabia, and Pakistan, maybe Afghanistan.

But, Precedent Bush, (I spelled it that way intentionally because he never really won the election. It was fraud and everyone knows it, and the Republicans went as far as having 'brown shirts' like Nazis stopping the voting. And, don't get me started on the Chad fraud). Bush, can't spell and can't think clearly through his alcoholic drenched and drug-impacted brain. He listened to others who lied to him and attacked Iraq, instead of going after his family's friend's son, Osama Bin Laden. Senior Bush, King George I, was in the petroleum business with the Bin Laden family, or didn't you know? King George the W went after the only dictator to threaten dear ole' dad's George Bush Sr.'s life. And that would be … Saddam Hussein. Hussein was just another dirty old man with a perverted son, and they both terrorized only their own people and later Kuwait.

We all know this to be true. Yet, nearly a trillion dollars was wasted on the Iraq war. And the takedown of Iraq opened the door for the creation of ISIS and for them to gain control; all good political analysts agree with that. And, besides that a vast majority of that money went into the pocket of VP Cheney and his cronies in the military complex to attack a former ally. But, but no one will ever bring them to Justice – and still the Republicans say today, Bush I and Bush II were good presidents, and that Ronald Reagan is the greatest living American President. That shows the depth of Republican ignorance, they don't even realize that Reagan's not living, he's dead.

Republicans are known for their stupidity and saying stupid things:

"Racism exists because we have a sin problem, not a skin problem."
– Gov. Mike Huckabee

"Who does Kanye think he is running for president?
What experience does he have? None."
– Donald Trump

"You watch a sonogram of a 15-week baby, and they have movements that are purposeful," (like masturbating)
- Republican Rep. Michael Burgess

Yes, to a Republican masturbating is purposeful.

And the winner of all times is …

"Climate Change Doesn't Exist, and If It Does It's Caused By Trees."

Their resistance to the very idea of climate change is so staunch that it bred an entire theory of GOP-specific ignorance. The least crazy of the party acknowledge climate change is occurring but refuse to link it to human behavior, instead seeing the rise in temperatures, more powerful hurricanes, cyclones, etc.

But the Republicans not only say stupid things ... their stupidity goes beyond that, i.e., arming the police for war. They send war surplus equipment to the Police. Then have the police declare war on all blacks in Ferguson, Missouri. But, I'm not really for peaceful solution for the police who do these murders or participate in murder squads.

I don't believe they should be negotiated with. I believe that a process of getting to the truth is needed: using sodium pentothol, lie detectors, hypnosis - whatever it takes to get to the truth. And, when it's discovered that the police murdered someone who was innocent, like in Baltimore or in Staten Island, New York, or even questionable Mike Brown in Ferguson, that police officer needs to get a bullet to the brain. Period!

It's like bringing back the guillotine - the bullet costs 25 cents, a year in prison costs between $30,000 to $150,000 per prisoner depending what state or city you are in – and the taxpayers pay for prisoners to be incarcerated. There are 3 million prisoners costing taxpayers billions of dollars. And since the prison system is basically privatized, Republican owners are getting rich.

Introduction

This book is simply a collection of essays I've written, plus some thoughts gathered into one easy source for people to access. It certainly doesn't cover every issue. It's about the current state of the United States, and its current free-fall from grace as the dominant power within the Western World as a source of Culture, Science, Freedom, and Inspiration. It's not a secret, and lots of Americans feel very same way. There is something seriously wrong with this good ole U.S. of A., and something needs to be done to bring it back on track before it's too late. But, it might already be too late.

While there are a lot of other things that could be done, and a lot of ways that have been enacted over the years from social movements such as the Occupy Wall Street movement to the Tea Party formation, none of them seem to have worked. In fact, there are still a lot of problems that plague our country, even now. All the way from how the United States has failed in education, with various European countries and even Third World countries outpacing us regarding quality and spirit of education, to the fact that our Prisoner population stands at an all-time high. Hell, we even out pace other nations that have been known to violate basic human rights in incarceration rates. That's right. There are dictatorships out there with lower incarceration rates than the United States.

And of course, all of that is a problem. That's not even mentioning the growing discontent of the citizens themselves as our own police force turns on us and uses strong-armed tactics to beat us to a pulp. In fact, within the last two years alone, we've seen a marked spike in fatalities performed by policemen that's caused a second wave of Civil Rights violations in the form of the "Black Lives Matter" movement because of the increase in police brutality incidents. These have resulted in an increase in various minority deaths, and it's not just an African American problem either that's growing but covering various social classes as well. It's a plague on American civil rights.

That's not to mention what the United States Government is doing with Congressional members wanting to de-fund, or outright abolish social programs. Medicaid, Medicare, Social Security, Planned Parenthood, Food Stamps, Welfare, Education, the Arts and Sciences, and all of that would be going away. Various members of Congress, both Conservative, and Liberal argue about how best to de-fund them, to put those dollars towards their different (mostly military) pet projects. All of which includes funding wars in the Middle East like our various battles in Afghanistan, Iraq, and the possibility of entering into Syria, and possibly Iran, and elsewhere at some point in time.

All of this, of course, costing taxpayers billions and billions of dollars per year without any benefit shown for their hard work and sacrifice in paying those taxes. Well, not all citizens of course. It's easy to see who truly benefit from this, as the top 1% of the United States seems to be perfectly fine paying less than half of what middle class wage earners pay in taxes. They keep getting richer by the minute as their corporations take over various different societal institutions such as prisons, schools, police stations, roadways, and government works because the Government cannot afford to keep its infrastructure working and up-to-date.

In the end, this book might seem overly harsh. At times, it might even seem extremely inflammatory. However, that only shows the passion that goes into the writing. At the end of the day, it is not just one man's anger at a society that is falling apart at the seams and forgetting the people who made this nation great at one point in time, but a collection of thoughts on how to best possibly fix the problems that are plaguing us. Still, the solution sometimes is only the cost of a bullet to the brain to get things back on track.

Naturally, violence only begets violence, and the writing within is rhetorical to that theme. As was stated before, in such incidents such as police murdering their own citizens, or a Congressional member was found to be corrupt in his dealings and not putting the Americans first, punishment is needed. Or, if a CEO of a company destroys lives and industry for profit, there's no sense in housing them in an overcrowded prison. It would cost the taxpayers who are already overburdened over $100,000 a year when you can pay a quarter for a bullet, and the $10 for a janitor for an hour's worth of work to mop up the blood and guts.

Harsh? True. But very fair as well.

It will take a lot of hard work and dedication to get this country back on track, that much is certain. It won't happen overnight, that much is true as well. However, it can be done once all of the citizens of the United States wake up from their apathetic daze and realize that the problems CAN be fixed with some simple applications. Vote out the crooks in Washington, you can recognize them easily – they are all the millionaires in Congress or have been in congress 12 years or longer. Vote in sensible laws, stop the wars in the Middle East, defund part of the Military budget to only what is necessary and reinvest the surplus in infrastructure, social conventions, education, and small businesses in the economy. Only care about foreign situations as it pertains to allies and international friends in the community. Only then can things get fully back on track.

Once all of that is taken care of … who's to say? No doubt things will once again get better for everyone. If things don't end up back on track fully, there's no telling what can happen, though we've seen what happened with the fall of Rome and inept governance. After all, those who ignore the lessons of history are doomed to repeat it, which should be a major lesson and a theme of this book besides a call to action.

CHAPTER 1
Propaganda and Partisanship

Part 1: Absolving the Two Party System

There is a prevalent problem in America today. A problem that goes far beyond what most of us tend to realize is actually happening. In a lot ways, it's become the root of the divisional factions we tend to have today between everyone. It's one of the major reasons that we cannot discuss politics without drawing dividing lines separating people and their opinions.

Since the foundation of this great Nation, our political system has largely been dominated by two major political parties that come to represent us in Congress, and it extends to almost all of the branches of our government today. Even today it still manages to dominate our politics and our current way of thinking, with political choices coming down to Democrats or Republicans.

This is a serious problem we face as a nation even today. First of all, there is a lot of inherent problems that come with having a two party system. Not only do we have to deal with the issue of our politics being colored in either red or blue whenever we have an opinion on things, but that also means that we have to make decisions based on which party aligns most closely with our opinions as well.

Anyone can see the major issue regarding this. We, as people, tend to have a wide range of opinions on a lot of things and have an idea on how best to run our nation.

> "Opinions are the blind and lazy alleys of stupid and
> foolish people who can't think for themselves."
>> - Ambrose Bierce (reportedly eaten by cannibals)

In fact, no two people will ever truly agree on anything, let alone everything, and the basis of Democracy is that we learn to compromise with one another. We learn to share ideas, debate with one another and discuss ways to improve our nation. However, the two party system tends to negate that sort of debate and instead creates an air of argumentation when it forces each of its adherents to follow in lock step with one another to vote down party lines. They two party system punishes any free thinker who moves even a step or two out of place.

Even if you agree on issues with the opposite party, if you're a Democrat you seemingly are not allowed to vote on any measures presented by a member of the Republican Party, and vice-versa.

However, that's exactly what politicians within Washington D.C want you to believe as well. Politicians expect people to stay within their respective parties because it makes it easier to manipulate them, hog tie them, and force them to be the next dinner.

Yes, control and manipulate! After all, if you know exactly what everyone is willing to follow, it makes it easier for manipulating the law for your own personal and financial advantages. Look at the background composition of most of the politicians and what careers they started out at. Lawyer, Lying, Lawyers! In fact over 90% of the time, politician's career background before they got into politics comes from studying the law to learn how to bend it, or even break it without being caught.

Rarely any scientists, any psychologists, or counselors, nor any doctors, nor any teachers, nor butcher, baker, or candlestick maker, or any other career that specializes in anything outside of studying the law, except lately one comedian. Or are they all comedians, they sure make us laugh with their stupid and idiotic comments. Yet, at the same time they somehow are expected to be able to make laws that deal with a diversity of subjects that they know nothing about while skirting them simultaneously.

For example, Republicans talking without knowing what the fuck they are talking about here's just one of thousands of examples:

"But we also know that the very founders that wrote those documents worked tirelessly until slavery was no more in the United States. ... I think it is high time that we recognize the contribution of our forbearers who worked tirelessly -- men like John Quincy Adams, who would not rest until slavery was extinguished in the country."
– *GOP presidential candidate Michele Bachmann, speaking at a 2011 Iowan's for Tax Relief event. The Founding Fathers did not work to end slavery, and John Quincy Adams was not one of the Founding Fathers.*

The politics of the US are a big problem. First, Republicans are generally ignorant, don't know history, hardly know the Bible they are forever spouting, and say the most ridiculous things. They ought to be on a Comedy stage in their local towns spewing their garbage or get on Saturday Night Live. - the editor.

There are several solutions to our political problems, but the question is whether or not people are willing to go that far to fix the current political climate that's affected American politics since its inception 240 years ago. The first thing that needs to be addressed is fixing the two party system that dominates all branches of our government. The Judicial, Legislative, and even Executive branches all vote along their respective parties line, even at the Supreme Court level or the Presidential positions where the law comes first. Or, the American people as a whole should take precedence over politics. But it doesn't. By eliminating our current two party system that dominates everything politically, we pave the path to allow more room for more voices and more opinions to be heard.

No longer constrained between "liberal" and "conservative", the political narrative can, instead, move from Democrat or Republican majority to then encompass people having different ideas to come to the table. If someone has a moderate view that takes both aspects of liberal idealism, and conservative pragmatism, they can no longer be viewed as an outcast by both parties, but can be voted in as they should have been in the first place.

In fact, among all of our founding fathers, George Washington favored this approach above all and has even warned that allowing Congress to be dominated by two parties would inevitably lead to disaster. How right he was, as not even 100 years after our nation's founding the United States splintered and fractured along party lines when Abraham Lincoln became President of the United States. At that moment, our nation was literally divided along two highly polarized point of view.

Plus, by absolving the two political party system, we also will end up with more honest politicians as honesty would soon become the norm for voting instead of being deceptive as politicians are today. By being open and honest with various constituents, they can garner more respect and admiration and even more votes as opposed to being as deceptive as they are (and I am talking to the Republican politicians specifically). They need to work within party lines to get what they want and their energy goes to screw the public and country out of what they really need.

Plus, with the elimination of the two party system, we can also get rid of the benefits for politicians as well. No more free rides for those that choose to go into the public sector and politics as a whole. Now, whatever law that they pass will apply to them as well. Under the Affordable Healthcare Act (Obamacare), these politicians would have to find a medical health provider they can trust with their health, instead of abusing the taxpayers' dollars to pay for their high-priced medical expenses at Walter Reed Medical Center.

So now, they can craft a bill that's good for the people, and not just argue about it endlessly with no idea of what it even contained. No longer will they be able to be provided a free (tax-free) campaign funding which they pocket personally, even if they lose. (Isn't that grand theft?)

No more life-time-long pensions (entitlements) for their time in Congress. No more bribery from lobbyists or political action committees to push through lobbyist or PAC actions that benefit corporations, industry, and/or private interests like the Big-Pharma industry, or the AMA, or the NRA, or McDonalds, Burger King, the Beef, Pork and Chicken industries.

The free ride must end, and we need to change how our system works for the betterment of our Nation, and the American people.

Part 2: The Fox News Propaganda Machine.

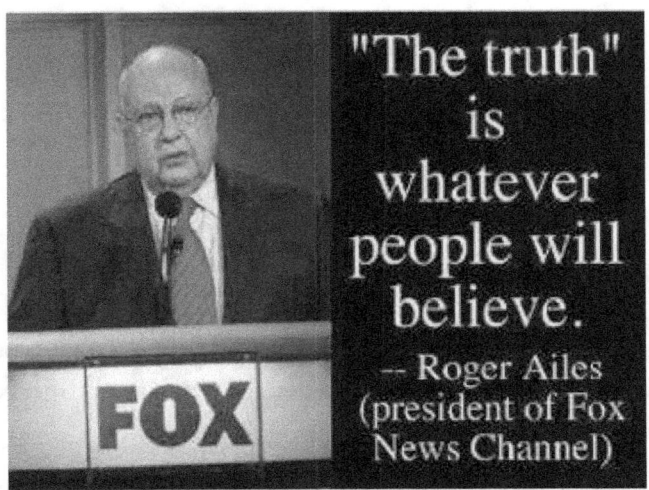

"The truth" is whatever people will believe.
-- Roger Ailes (president of Fox News Channel)

Fox News. They lie, they lie, they lie.

What more could truly be said of the venerated news program that airs not only on its own channel for cable television in 24 hours news cycle much like CNN, MSNBC, BBC and other's that can be bought with a basic cable package. Not much, more than likely given by the fact that since it has become one of the most popular news networks within the United States, a lot of people have had a lot of things to say about it.

One woman, who had left her parents' home to begin her career, returned home to find her parents riveted to Fox News and were almost deranged with anger against President Obama and Democrats, to a point where she thought if they had a gun, her parents would begin a killing spree. That rings of hypnotic negative programming – and when watching Fox News, I find that they are forever saying downright evil things – like all the blacks deserved to die, that slavery wasn't that bad, in fact, it was an educational experience, and having guests misquoting the Bible. I am in shock that this trash is allowed on the air, but concerned that it enrages people to a point of getting guns and shooting people. - the editor.

Fox News supporters claim that its conservative slant is a major counterweight to the supposedly liberal ideology of other cable networks currently on air. But, detractors claim that it often skews the news for a Republican political agenda and one that unfairly targets liberals or even moderate people through the use of illogical fallacies. *I call this outright lies. – the editor.* Whether or not you agree with any of the statements said in favor or against the network, a lot of people can agree that at its core, Fox News is more than just a news show, but also a tool used for propaganda misused by the Republican Party, who controls it.

It's easy to see why as well. The News, for the most part, is supposed to be unbiased in how they present information. Journalists and Newspapers and News programs at its core are simply supposed to present the events and facts to the public. Period! They're supposed to do it without any hint of bias in their reporting. They are supposed to allow the citizens who learn what they have to say make their own decision. Fox News doesn't do that.

But, that's the intent behind journalism. The problem that Fox News presents is that since its inception in 1996, it has proven only capable of creating news and framing it around the ideal of their opinions and thoughts. They frame it to an audience and hinting to their audience on what they should believe. They tell their audience what they should think when it comes to the news that they created or misrepresented.

In fact, at one point in time, Fox News went on the record to say that anything that they present shouldn't be taken purely as news, but "opinions about the news" as presented to the public to disseminate the information for consumption instead.

All of the previous statements made about Fox News should be a reason to completely disregard anything reported by the Fox News Network. But, it actually goes deeper than that in how Fox News is biased in how it presents information for viewers. They frame the news as an agenda.

Just look at who owns the Network and controls it completely: Rupert Murdoch. The Australian Business Magnate, who is the Chairman and CEO of the global media holding company News Corporation, which is the world's largest Media Conglomerate.

In fact, Rupert Murdoch owns not only Fox News but newspapers (including the Wall Street Journal). He also has competing shares in other major Networks (some even in competition) and has shown that he's willing to leverage all of that media power for his own personal gains. In fact, Fox News itself was first created after former Republican Party media consultants were hired to form the basis of the Fox News channel despite the fact that Fox News employees insist that they act without bias in their presentation of the news. Yeah sure.

Of course, those statements from employee's neglect the fact that Fox News itself has been caught several times over the years blatantly misrepresenting facts, fabricating quotes and poll numbers, misconstruing facts to serve their agenda, and using photos, video, and quotes out of context to drum up support. *(Liar, Liar, Catch on Fire – the editor.)*

Not only that, but they've also used argumentative fallacies (lies) hundreds or thousands of times to deny or outright ignore claims made by scientists, liberals, or other educated specialists. One of the most egregious examples of this sort of distortion happened in 2009. That occurred when Fox News employee Gregg Jarret reported on a Sarah Palin book signing in Grand Rapids, Michigan. Jarret reported that there was as massive turnout to the event, neglecting the pictures and video footage shown on Fox News was from the previous year during the McCain-Palin campaign rally. And, when Fox got caught with their pants down, claimed it was a "video error" instead.

One of their outright, biggest lies, came during the 2004 President Campaign when Fox News misled viewers into showing fabricated quotes (more lies) that they attributed to John Kerry. But claimed, after they had been caught with their pants down, that the quotes came from an article that was on their own website and was intended to be a joke article … and never meant to be shown. The damage was already done. Why weren't they sued for slander? *Probably because the judges are Republicans also! - the editor.*

There are, of course, more incidents that Fox News is guilty off that show that it's nothing more than the propaganda machine of the Republican Party. *(They lie, they lie, they lie – about everything, does that make it clearer – the editor).*

None of this is more evident than their coverage of everything that the now current President, Barack Obama, does while in office. It's even gotten to the point that the President can't scratch his ass without it being declared an issue from the Fox News Network. It ranges from Steve Doocy, mocking the President using a binder clip, to the "terrorist fist jab" line that E.D Hill said when Barack Obama's fist bumped his wife, Michelle. Then it goes to a "Psychiatrist" on the show to claim that Barack Obama was victimized by his parents and is only seeking the Presidential seat to take it out on the United States.

Of course that even doesn't begin to describe the entire "birther" movement with Fox News claiming that the President was an illegal Muslim Kenyan and, therefore, unqualified to run for the Presidential Seat. (They lie, they lie, they lie.) But they do nothing about Ted Cruz, who wasn't born in the United States. He's Canadian. Prejudiced news network that protects criminals – that's Fox News.

The propaganda even extends to issues of race as well as it shows fully how insensitive the employees of the Fox News Network are when it comes to race and gender. One major example comes from an episode of the show "Hannity" that aired in June of 2013 when Sean Hannity had right wing radio host Bill Cunningham on the show, and the discussion turned to Attorney General Eric Holder committing perjury. No sooner has commentator Tamara Holder opened her mouth to give her opinion than Bill Cunningham yelling to "Shut up, know your role, and shut your mouth." Further attacking her via ad hominem when he stated "What, are you going to cry?" and calling her a liberal stooge. There's even been times they've had people come onto their Network shows to speak down of the LGBT community by comparing them to NAMBLA because of their identified sexuality. And, then talks about other races when Fox News employee Brian Kilmeade claimed that American's aren't pure because its citizens kept "marrying other species and other ethnics." *Other species – come on! – the editor.*

The saddest part of all of this is that there are many more incidents like the above where they attack anything that does not fit on the conservative Born-Again, Christian, Republican agenda that they continue to extol.

No one seems to care either, which only makes it more sad as the Fox News network currently holds a majority of the market share, and airs currently in over 85% of basic cable television homes, and commands over a million followers. That, of course, means that there are a lot of people out there who listen, follow, repeat, and propagate the dribble that Fox labels as news.

Not only that, it appears the followers of Fox News get violent over hearing that Fox News content is a lie. They even get angry when their educated children tell them that they are listening to prejudiced lies.

Hopefully, in time, the citizens of the United States will wake up and realize the foolishness of listening to this cable news network and realize they're being spoon fed opinions instead of allowing them to have true News only networks. Hopefully soon, as Americans have the power to break the cycle of propaganda and can realize they can form their own opinions after all.

Part 3: The Brainlessness of the Republican Candidates for Presidency

How quickly time seems to fly. It almost seems strange that almost 8 years ago we were in the midst of an election year, with the two dominating parties of the American Government locked in a heated battle. On the one side, we had the then Senator Barack Obama on the Democratic ticket, his message of hope and change energizing an entire nation into coming out and voting for him, and re-energizing the youth of the nation into getting up and caring for the democratic process of voting. At the same time, on the Republican Ticket we had the Senator John McCain, his political opponent who ran on the issues of how he was a better candidate for the presidency by being an old, white, crotchety, prisoner of war.

To balance out his antiquity, and his grumpiness he ran with the then Governor of Alaska, Sarah Palin, whom it seemed had the uncanny knack of opening her mouth, inserting her foot and having the dumbest things just seemingly spew out of it all the time wherever she went. Sounding like an idiot who had too much to drink. She was completely bereft of intelligence or trust.

Unsurprisingly, Senator Barack Obama won in an almost landslide against his opponent McCain, becoming not only the first African American President but almost one of the youngest Presidents this Nation has ever seen.

Time seems to change for the most part since then. 2008 seemingly like a lifetime ago. We've seen a lot of things happen in that time, a lot of political up and downs, a lot of turmoil and all, and a lot of wins and losses. For the most part, we've pulled ourselves out from Iraq, managed to not go to war with Iran, remained in Afghanistan, but starting to draw the Middle Eastern wars to a close. Not only that, but we've seen the death of Osama Bin Laden, the Arab Spring, the burst of the housing bubble and it's recovery, as well as the strengthening of the European Union until Greece bottomed up on its debt and defaulted of course.

However, the one thing that has not changed at all was Congress itself, as usual. The mandate, since Barack Obama took office away from the Republican part of the aisle, has deliberately been "Stop Obama at all cost, and then blame him for our own incompetency." This is a bold tactic utilized by anyone but was taken to extreme with the Republican majority congress since 2010, when the Republicans won back both houses of Congress.

Since then, any movement that even has a hint of support for the President has been blocked, time and time again while the Republicans threaten to filibuster or close down the government completely, making veterans and poor people starve. In fact, who can forget easily how long the fight over the so called "Obamacare" has been going on? Since its inception, which is startlingly since Obamacare is nothing more than a repackaged concept that the Republicans themselves had created in the 90's, and early 2000's ubiquitously titled "Romneycare" as it was devised by the Massachusetts Congressman. The only real difference is that it's been titled "Obamacare" despite the fact its real name is "The Affordable Care Act", which the Republicans should have ate up, jumped on the bandwagon, and laid claim to having devised it. Instead, because they didn't want President Obama "to win", they fought against their own creation tooth and nail, each and every time.

Of course, the most damning part of it all is when they shut down the Government in October of 2013 because the Republican led Congress didn't want to pass the budget that year. They didn't want to do that because the President called for cuts in several different sections of the budget, even though those sections were chosen specially by a non-partisan Committee made up of both Democrats and Republicans both, who agreed on it.

However, since the President himself had endorsed it, they decided that they had no need of the budget and decided instead to draft up a counter budget proposal. All of their counter proposal would have gutted much needed social programs, such as Child Services, Federally run Hospitals, Schools, Federal Aid, Welfare, and most damning of all, Veteran Benefits. The very same people, at the same time, they were touting as heroes and putting upon pedestals for their own selfish gains.

Naturally, Democrats, long champion of social welfare and benefits to the poorest of society did not agree to the budget change at all, and they entered into a deadlock, wanting to stick to the original budget. When it failed to pass, Republicans then blamed the President for its failure, despite the fact that it's Congress's job to vote and enact the budget while the President simply signs the bill. Republicans simply wanted to cut off their nose to spite their faces and blame it all on President Obama. And that is simply one issue of many that have cropped up over the years where the Republicans have blocked every single attempt for any sort of change from the President. Welfare, Diplomacy, even pardoning the White House Turkey during the Thanksgiving feast has been blocked, debated, and ridiculed by Congressional Republicans.

And now, here we are, close to another election year. And, all of the Republicans now have come out of the woodwork to claw, and clamber over each other, arguing, spitting in each other's eyes, and otherwise acting in buffoonery manner. They are all doing this in the name of winning the coveted position of running for President of the United States on the Republican ticket in the 2016 election. The biggest issue, however, is that it would seem that the only people in this upcoming election cycle are the idiots of the party. The Republicans having invested so much time, so much energy, and so much of their vitriol against President Obama, Gays, Democrats, and Liberals that they hadn't had the time to sweep their skeletons under the carpet, and hide the dumbness.

In fact, it would almost seem that a hodgepodge of the crazies have come out to ask to be our next leader, which is sad considering that none of them have ever truly led anything other than a congressional circus. Most of them are simply known for being contrarian buffoons, with a lot of their own accomplishments, since 2008, having been nothing but "I've prevented the President from doing his job while not doing mine either."

Breaking down, of course, the Presidential Candidates, we can also discuss what it is about them that would make them entirely unsuitable for the jobs at hand.

First up in the line of Republican Presidential hopefuls is Jeb Bush. One of the top five front runners of the 2016 election season it would seem, because I suppose the Republicans forgot what happened the last two times a Bush was in the White House. Still, Jeb Bush is surprisingly more articulate than his brother, George Bush, Jr., but it would seem he's no stranger to the anti-President Obama culture that the Republicans in Congress wish to perpetuate on a daily basis.

In fact, a lot of times Jeb Bush might seem folksy in comparison, but he's still woefully incompetent when it comes to anything. Not only has Florida, a location prime for its tourism industry fail to turn a profit under his watch, but he also seems to be lax on getting the Memo's. When the Obama administration decided to close down the Vatican Embassy, and move it closer to the Holy See, instead of waiting for confirmation or asking, he decided to make up facts and claim that the Obama administration did that to punish Catholics who were against Obamacare.

Not only was he wrong on both accounts, but in truth, a lot of Catholics are actually supportive of social welfare reform to help the poor and needy. I suppose Jeb Bush, like his brother, forgot what Jesus's message truly is.

The next in line for discussion practically needs no introduction, as his hair tends to be the first thing that enters the room and then stupid conversation followed with his ego. Donald Trump seemingly crawled out of the bottom of the luxurious bridge he was doing double-duty on as a troll, to one more run to become the President of the United States. A task he's performed since 2004. However, the problem with Donald Trump running for President isn't just that he's orange. He squints like he's looking into the sun and has a huge ego problem. But mostly, he's corrupt, has a mental disorder called narcissism. Everything is all about Donald Trump squeaks megalomaniac all the time.

Recently, he's come under fire for his comments regarding Immigrants from Mexico, claiming that all of them defacto, are criminals, and meaning to cause us harm through criminal activity. Not only has he lost sponsors because of his commentary, but his reply to the whole fiasco is "I'm right, you're wrong, and I'm going to sue you".

Then, he's turned around and sued various sponsors of his who did not agree with his statement, and stopped sponsoring him or partnering with them because of his race-baiting remarks of hatred for others.

Another Republican, who has thrown in their hat into the ring, of course, is Congressman Chris Christie, who believes that he has what it takes to become the next President of the United States. Not realizing of course that New Jersey goons went out of style in the 1930's, especially the really fat ones.

Still, the problem with Chris Christie manifests mostly in the fact that while he had developed a lot of goodwill towards many, including sometimes reaching across the aisle to Democrats, and working with President Obama, he often was out of step with Republican idealism for the sake of what was good for his constituents. Then, he squandered any of that goodwill when he used his political clout like a cudgel against Fort Lee's Mayor Mike Sokolich and shut down the George Washington State Bridge all in an attempt to politically damage Mayor Mike, who did not endorse him.

Of course, Chris Christie was never indicted on the charges of corruption, and his aides instead took the fall for his actions, the American People and the People of New Jersey are not as stupid as Christie himself.

That goes hand-in-hand with the insensitivity of Canadian-born Senator Ted Cruz, another potential hopeful for the White House and by law should not be able to run for office due to being foreign-born. The most damning thing about the man is his attitude towards any political opponent. He deems unworthy of having a sensitive bone in his body. Having a problem with constantly inserting his foot in his mouth, Senator Ted Cruz found it funny, and hilarious to seek out Joe Biden while the Vice President was in mourning over the death of his son, Beau, and at the same time claim "Vice President Joe Biden, you know the nice thing? You don't need a punch line," before Vice President Joe Biden has any chance to fully work out his grief with his family. A low blow from an insensitive clod who has no regard for the feelings of others. Perhaps, he should stick to what he normally does best; basking in the glory of White Castle Burgers and talking about Green Eggs and Ham.

Still, while Senator Ted Cruz is at least insensitive to the pain of others whom he might look down upon, that doesn't compare to the utter stupidity of Senator Lindsey Graham, who enjoys his time in the spotlight enough that it apparently has affected his hearing, and his brain function. The problem with Lindsey Graham stems mostly from the fact that while he works on Capitol Hill, and within the government, he has no idea of how Government actually works. In fact, during budget meetings several years ago before the Government shut down, he claimed that Medicaid, Medicare, and Social Security are all "entitlements" that should be cut to preserve the budget and balance it. He forgot that 1- we paid for it and 2 - those sections of Welfare constitute less than 5% of the total budget combined. Then, simultaneously he claimed that budget cuts shouldn't affect the outrageous Congressional entitlements like over-priced pensions, and high-priced Congressional medical coverage because those two were separate things.

However, perhaps his stupidity regarding where the money of the Budget goes can be explained by his recent joke that he plans to have "an all Jewish Cabinet," because as he had joked, Jews certainly know how to make money and keep it.

Granted, that at the time, the Senator was drunk. But, now we all know what sort of a person he is because when inebriated sloppy drunks tend to tell their true feelings.

Then there is Dr. Ben Carson, who is always looking down, never looking into people's eyes, who refuses to call Barack Obama a Black President, and telling ties of his sponsorship of a vitamin and nutrient company that he was deeply involved in that was involved in frauds and scandal. In addition, he's been saying stupid things about the Pyramids of Egypt being built to store grain. He says it's in the Bible – it's not. Do you think the Egyptians would bury their dead with their citizen's food supply? Are we going to elect an idiot to office?

So these are just a few small samplings of the Republicans that feel they deserve to be sitting in the White House come the November 2016 election. And, as we have seen, none of them are worthy of the title of President, as all seemingly are more focused on their own fame and fortune, their own power, and how much time in the Fox News they can grab. Honestly, it's like Netflix's "House Of Cards", played to the tune of Yakkety Sax in the background on auto-repeat.

Other Presidential hopefuls include the alumni of the Republican ideology of "don't let Obama do anything". That includes other Republican congressmen such as Bobby Jindal, Mike Huckabee, Rand Paul, and even Mitt Romney once more on the ticket to try and see if he can continue to salvage his dignity from the last Presidential Race from insulting the 47%. *Losers and Liars ALL! — the editor.*

Should any of those go to the Podium as the defacto choice come the Election Cycle, God help any Americans when it comes time to vote.

Part 4: Donald Trump – The Donald

Sometimes, that feels like that's all that needs to be said about the Donald, really. Conjuring his name brings a lot of images to mind. Some of it good, a lot of it not so good. Wild orange hair, orange skin, fake personality, reprehensible, looks like a gnarly scrotum, and all sorts of things come to mind when the name gets mentioned anywhere. And in these days of politics, people are more divided than ever on the man and his political stances. Why, though often, becomes the question, especially considering the sort of person that Donald Trump is, and the things that he says.

While it's not hard to understand since he speaks more to a baser desire on certain aspects, it's actually hard to understand why people, especially lower-income people, would even want to vote for the man given the sort of person that he is.

Forget all of his politics and put that aside while focusing on his business and personality, it makes it even more mind-boggling as to why he's often been leading the polls. Is America stupid?

Trump has always been rich, there's no doubt about that. He's never had to really work a day in his life. Sure, he's probably had late nights where he's had to talk and drink with a lot clients and other interested parties, and there's no doubt that he's had to learn what he's learned to get ahead. After all, no one can build a fortune from a million dollar loan from his father than he never repaid, and not be at least intelligent in some way. But with Donald Trump, he's never had to do manual labor. He's never sweated for what he's earned, he's never had to hit rock bottom, and he's never had to know what it's like working outside in 90+ degree weather or working in the mud and dust to make what he's currently got.

Currently, he's 69 years old, but he actually got his start in life early on when he began working for his father's real estate company "Elizabeth Trump and Son" in 1968. His father's company wasn't exactly a small time business organization either, as "Elizabeth Trump and Sons" oversaw condo and home development in the NYC, and at the time pulled in millions of dollars. Just three years later, after officially joining, he was given complete control of the company and renamed it "The Trump Organization" after himself. In the 80's, he mostly spent his time investing in other real estate and expanding The Trump Organization with various different hotels, and other buildings that got turned around.

Several times, he ran afoul of the Justice Department between the 70's and late 80's due to the Fair Housing Act. Still, it wasn't until the start of the millennium that Donald Trump became a household name thanks to a string of Reality Television shows featuring him. The most noticeable of which was "The Apprentice" where people competed against each other for a chance to intern in his organization which spawned the catchphrase "You're Fired".

However, it's his other ventures outside of real estate development that got him noticed a lot more. And, (rightfully so), with a mountain of criticism. While Donald Trump knows Real Estate better than anyone, despite having always had the money to do so, the same cannot be said of his other investments. In 1988 for example, Donald Trump acquired the Taj Mahal Casino and quickly started to lose money, increasing his overall debt with the casino.

In fact, it wasn't even a full year before Trump was unable to meet the loan payments he took out to acquire the Casino, and by 1991 forced Trump to declare bankruptcy on the Casino and restructure it. In the process, he lost more than half of his ownership in the business as well as other businesses he had acquired or built up in the process. That included his "Trump Shuttle" airline, and a yacht named "The Trump Princess."

His other failed business ventures, of course, included ownership of a Football team from the mostly defunct "United States Football League (USFL) and only minor success with being a part owner of the Miss Universe Beauty Pageant since 1996. But then, in 2015 he opened his big mouth and NBC and Univision, as well as other sponsors, ended their business relationships with Trump *(because of the pure bullshit he's been saying about Mexico. – the editor.)*

It wasn't until 2011 that Trump officially started a political career. Sure, before that, he'd done a lot of work in donation to charity organizations, as well as candidates that he endorsed both Republican and Democratic. However, it wasn't until the second decade of the new millennium that he decided to enter into the Presidential race as a front runner.

However, in the lead up to the 2012 election he lost out to other Republican hopefuls, and eventually supported Mitt Romney's election in February of 2012. Earlier, in April of 2011, Trump started off the current cycle of stating stupid things when he questioned President Barack Obama's proof of citizenship, claiming that Obama was Kenyan since birth and wasn't a citizen while living in Hawaii.

Even now he continues to make claims against the President that aren't based on his policies, but on ad hominin attacks and straw men used to divert attention from other serious issues, and bringing the discussion back to Trump himself.

This seems to be the case with the current 2016 President Elections that are going on now with Trump as the current front runner of the GOP, currently leading the polls among conservative Americans. It's actually a major wonder why such a man could be considered for President given that he not only looks like an angry old wrinkled gerbil, but also his words and political stances are completely reprehensible and outlandishly stupid when you sit down to actually consider them. First and foremost, he can't play nice. He's rich, with a net worth of over an estimated $4 to 8 billion in accumulated wealth although he sometimes claims $10 billion. But Donald Trump, himself, is incapable of talking about the issues at hand. He often resorts to illogical fallacies that take away from the issues he's supposed to be talking about. Instead, he chooses to attack his opponents' character instead of their stances. Such as what he's had to say in regards to Republican Presidential candidate Carly Fiorina:

> "Look at that face! Would anyone vote for that?
> Can you imagine that, the face of our next President
> I mean, she's a woman, and I'm not supposed
> to say bad things, but really, folks, come on.
> Are we serious?"
>
> – *Donald Trump*

Where instead of citing her political ideology, he chose instead to make fun of her appearance and claim that she's invalidated as a candidate to him because she's not attractive, and she's a woman. All the while, he himself, looks like a wrinkled scrotum in a suit, but that's beside the point. To Donald Trump if he can attack a person's appearance, he feels he can somehow invalidate them. Of course, he can't go after integrity, which is pretty hard for someone who doesn't have any themselves.

At the same time, though, when you get down to what it is that Donald Trump himself believes you can see why he wants to divert attention away from that when doing debates with others. He only believes in his money, not even in his general scumbagginess while in front of a camera. One of the most prolific things he's debated, talked, and attacked people on in this election cycle as of this writing has been his stance on Mexico in general, and immigration reform. Quoted recently as saying:

"The U.S has become a dumping ground for everybody else's problems. When Mexico sends its people, they're not sending their best. They're not sending you. They're sending people that have lots of problems, and they're bringing those problems with us. They're bringing drugs. They're bringing crime. They're Rapists, and some I assume, are good people."

Mexican doesn't send its people, they come looking, on their own, for a better life, dumbass. - *the editor.*

And of course, talking about how, once he's won the General Election for President, he plans to erect a wall on the southern border to keep Mexicans from crossing the border into the United States and make Mexico pay for it. *In reality, if Trump were my neighbor I'd erect a wall and pay for it myself. – the editor.*

Naturally when anyone, with half a mind, criticized Trump for his words by claiming it was derogatory, he attacked back, claiming that what he's said was "correct", and that anyone who argues against him either is delusional or has some sort of economic reason to disagree with him. Of course, the backlash has been critical, but the sad fact of the matter is, it has not slowed him down as among all the Republican Candidates he still leads them in the polls. None of the other candidates currently have the exposure that Trump has, and sadly that's playing into the man's hands as that is more than likely the strategy used to garner attention.

Of course, thankfully, that's a double-edged sword, as other than his prejudicial views on Mexicans, he's completely empty on other stances. When quoted about his plan to add jobs to the United States economy, all he had to say was "*I will be the greatest jobs President that God ever created.*" which didn't really explain much, but at least it showed his megalomania.

Honestly, the entirety of The Donald can be summarized as a sad condition of the American Political system. It shows the utter lack in faith that Americans have in their political system that they let in a sleaze-ball with money have the chance to come in and have a general chance at winning the election. It's no surprise, Trump is pretty good with his money, and he knows how to make wealth even when he's losing, but that does not equate to running a country, and he's shown that he's generally pretty stupid in other areas outside of business.

He has no inner filter to keep his mouth shut, he rants, raves, is prejudicial, misogynistic, and even conservatives that aren't completely to the right of the political spectrum think he's a joke. But he's a symptom of a broken system where candidate after candidate has been so lackluster that the Media circus has to encircle him and wait for Donald Trump to open his mouth before endlessly talking about it. It's tiring and only serves to make the United States, further, the laughing stock of the world.

Donald Trump doesn't have to be elected President to be given the chance to fail and start the decline of the United States as a super power. The mere fact that he's relevant shows how far we've fallen, ad how irrelevant the United States is on a global scale. Donald Trump even being a serious

37

contender for President is exactly the herald of the fall of our democracy that some say is needed.

So what can we do? Sadly, in the end there's not much that can be done other than ignore Donald Trump, laugh at how dumb he looks, and ignore the fart noises that come from him that equate to his opinions. Hopefully in the end a candidate will step up from among the ranks and actually do the right thing and bring Politics back to what it's supposed to be about… not a three-ring circus for personalities, but debating on how best to lead this nation.

CHAPTER II

Our Fatal Foreign Policy

Part 1: Bush and Cheney, and the Profit off the Backs of the American Soldier.

2003 was a long time ago. As of now, roughly 12 years ago, and in a lot of ways it feels like it was in another lifetime. Things seemed a lot different back then. Not only was the Internet younger, fresher in everyone's mind, not as popular as it was now, but pop culture was vastly different. The technologies that we now take for granted hadn't even been developed. Not to mention that the Nation was still reeling from the effects of 9/11, the events not even 2 years old at that point. The cleanup of the rubble pile still going on. Not only that, but we were in the midst of a war in Afghanistan with the Taliban, whom we believed trained the 9/11 airplane hijackers, and who were connected to the Al-Qaeda and Osama Bin Laden network.

We were also in the midst of discussion of declaring war on Iraq and finishing the job there. The war rhetoric from President George Bush Jr and his administration was that we needed to go there to end terrorism, claiming that Saddam Hussein housed weapons of mass destruction (WMD's) and that he had them aimed to attack American soil, and other American Interests in the Middle East. That he also had chemical warfare capabilities, the same he had used against the Kurd's years earlier in the Northern part of Iraq. While saber rattling was going on, on the homefront, George Bush knew he had to have the approval of Congress to enact and declare war on Iraq.

Bush, illegally, bypassed this approval process for the sake of this war, and on March 20th, 2003 military operations officially began against Iraq with a coalition of NATO members from Great Britain, Australia, and a few other countries. They invaded Iraq on several different fronts from Kuwait, and surrounding nations.

At first, everything seemed to be going well. We believed we were disposing of a dictator, who was known for gassing his own citizens because they were from a different ethnic group than him, and we knew he was capable of all sorts of violence and abuses regarding human rights. Not only were we being heroes by avenging those we lost in the 9/11 attacks because we were told that Saddam Hussein was the power behind 9/11. *This was another Republican lie. – the editor.* But, we were liberating an area of the world that needed to see the goodness of democracy, and a chance to live a good life. We were going to win the hearts and minds of the Iraqis and no one would die in vain. All according to the Presidential plan. Ha!

Eventually, however, problems began to arise with the war in Iraq. To begin, we went in under the premise that Saddam had weapons of mass destruction. *(He did not. - The editor).* And, that he had weapons that were capable of reaching us. *(He did not. - the editor).* And, that they comprised of biological weaponry that included diseases such as anthrax, or worse. *(He didn't have any of that. – the editor.)* And, that if he used them he could cause a pandemic. *(But, he couldn't use what he didn't have. – the editor.)*

Not only that, we were told that he had chemical weapons including mustard gas and Sarin toxins, and it was the same that he used against the Kurd's. *(Nope! – the editor)*. And, that if unleashed on us could suffocate us to death, or even worse. *(No, siree! – the editor)*. That also included, of course, conventional explosive weaponry. *(Well, he had a little of that; every country does! – the editor)*.

Then, it was suggested, by the Bush administration, that Saddam was close to nuclear capabilities, and at his earliest opportunity chance he'd unleash it on us. *(Not even one nuclear facility under construction. – the editor)*.

As it turned out, there were no WMD's stockpiled. None within any cache of military equipment that was seized. And, we searched every square foot of Iraq and never found any. *(Lies, lies, lies, lies, lies. – the editor)*.

The result was disastrous. This was coupled with the war, at its onset being illegal to begin with, as Congress had not approved it. After Congress drafted a bill that allowed the President to declare war on Iraq, much later on, the war began looking less like a heroic effort of vengeance for 9/11 and liberation of the people. It was really looking more like a mad grab as large US corporations started to line up and take control of the vast oil fields within Iraq before a new government could even be established.

True, though, that we did come in and achieve a lot of the objectives that we had originally came to achieve. For starters, who could forget of the drama that unfolded when we were searching for Saddam Hussein? We had already killed and eliminated his sons, who were holed up with supporters of the Hussein regime and fighting to the last man already before we assassinated them.

Saddam Hussein, who seemed all powerful to the Iraqi people, was found hiding in a spider hole of sorts behind a barn, with barely any electricity. He no access to information for the most part. He was looking less and less like the monster of Baghdad and more and more like a lost and frightened old grandfather who had lost his way in life.

Who could forget the moment that President George Bush thought it was a good idea to fly out to an aircraft carrier for a photo op, choosing to wear a flight suit. He flew in on a jet and posed in front of a banner that was titled "Mission Accomplished".

Of course he forgot, then, that American soldiers were still fighting and dying in Iraq (where he was so far away from), because they were still taking out remnants of Saddam loyalists, and Al-Qaida operatives who certainly were issuing a fatwa against the invading army to fight a holy war.

Who could have perceived that we went into Iraq without an exit strategy? The American Government would still be in Iraq fighting and dying for nothing more than what was sold to us as a lie. The truth of the matter was that Iraq had nothing to do with 9/11 at all, and instead was slowly starting to crumble from within already. No WMD's, barely a fighting military, a nation nearly broke after selling off their oil, and of course with no relation to the 9/11 hijackers who were Saudi Arabian, and not Iraqi at all. And people blame Barack Obama for this war – UNBELIEVABLE!

Twelve years later, what do we have to show for it? Well, we're still fighting in Iraq - 4,487 American soldiers died since the onset of the War (with over an additional 2,000 having died in Afghanistan). That's over four thousand lives that have been lost in this war that we did not even need to be in, and we were sold on a lie to get us into it. Not to mention the illegality of it all. Yes, we, America, are the terrorists in this action.

Also being drawn into war before being properly written as a law, that's an imprisonable offense – but not for Bush and Chaney. They should be charged with war crimes.

Only after the fact that military action had been taken, the Congress made it a legal war with a Gung Ho attitude. Now, those figures do not include soldiers of other NATO member countries, nor the loss of human lives of innocent Iraqis. Mass murder was involved. And, no one takes into account the massive U.N humanitarian aid afterwards.

Besides the number of soldiers killed – many more were injured or maimed. The number of those either triples or quadruples the fatalities. Missing limbs - hands, legs, and eyes are reported as among a list of the injuries that are numbered among those that survived. Plus, there's no true statistic of the number of mental issues that veterans have suffered during combat, especially in high risk battle zones such as the city of Fallujah.

PTSD, nightmares, substance addiction problems, and an inability to integrate themselves back into civilian society after returning from their multiple tours have all led to severe problems that no one can truly enumerate because they are lacking physical evidence of the impact on a soldier's body.

Now, there were many thousand Iraqi civilian casualties who were caught in the middle between American soldiers, and insurgents who put pressure on the citizens by threatening violence if they helped the Americans. Then the Americans learned to distrust the civilians because of it after they had established a good relationship with them and the problems had reduced by about 85%.

The worst part of all of this, though, is that those in a position of power have profited the most from it all. Dick Cheney, Vice President, was still connected to a company he had led before, Halliburton, who took control of a majority of the oil fields in Iraq and over time used that oil to funnel money and power to various other companies Halliburton had control over. In fact, at the time of the Iraq War Dick Cheney was still drawing a paycheck as part of his "pension" from Halliburton, and even had stocks, bonds, and other such investments in Halliburton. He had a vested interest in this war, a criminal offense – but never prosecuted. He became a multi-multimillionaire from the military action.

By law, an official cannot hold ownership in any corporation doing business with the US government or armed forces.

Of course, there were crony companies of Dick Cheney and his Military Industrialized Complex and members in Congress who wanted this war to begin. Because as soon as the fighting started to die down they were there to profit from the setting up and rebuilding of Iraq. An entire industry between security (Blackwater), construction and oil (Halliburton), telecommunications, and more all sprung up around Iraq to prosper from rebuilding. The majority of those companies being tied to U.S. government officials who were either receiving campaign donations, "gifts", or who had a stake one way or another in the rebuilding effort.

This is all criminal activity going on in our government making legislators millionaires, illegally. In fact, the total sum of money that was made off the fighting came in the billions, with Dick Cheney himself having made millions off of it.

Illegal and unacceptable, something must be done about it – but never will be done because it's all Republican criminal activity. This has set a horrible precedent that Governments can destroy another one based on tangential connections through the use of rhetoric and propaganda, essentially lies and misinformation, to get what they want. And it's just convenient that we invaded a country that was innocent of misdoing simply because they happened to be in the same neighborhood of the world as Osama Bin Laden.

Of course, we can all agree that Saddam Hussein was a horrible human being, after all ... he threatened the life of glorious King George Bush, the senior, and that the government he had established was destructive to its own citizens. But, it was still stable and the bloodshed that it enacted was nowhere near the bloodshed that went on through our declaring war on Iraq who was innocent of wrong-doing in 9/11 and WMD's.

Looking at the past, and knowing how our mismanagement of Iraq upon exit left Iraq open for the development of ISIS. The first thing that we as Americans need to do is get the hell out of Iraq completely. Leave it behind after destroying ISIS with our allies power and our own before they take over the world. Then, we can withdraw all our soldiers. No, we would not even leave a peacekeeping force. We could simply allow the combined efforts of NATO, and the United Nations to get involved in the rebuilding efforts of the nation at a no profit, and to keep the peace in the country until it is stabilized enough to stand on its own two feet.

It's worked in the past with WWII nations such as Germany, and Japan, and while we do still have military bases in those countries, they're not tied to any military conflict in the region. And, more or less, are just a sort of rotation for our military.

As has been the precedent when other nations get involved, we help them, as a whole grow to become giants of industry. Germany leading the EU with its economy, and Japan leading in technology throughout the world, are due to the US helping them grow post-war. That's not a bad policy at all.

But, what about the war profiteers. What should be done is -- the confiscation of all money that's been created through unjust means from persons and corporations, and all that is earned through the rebuilding process as well. Not, of course, for those people who actually do the work post-war, but the confiscation should be done for the Political leaders who called for the war in the first place, and that money instead be used for a good cause. That might be an investment in the Republic of Iraq's economy since most of that money was their money to begin with which was stolen through political and military manipulation.

In my belief, reparations should be repaid to the American soldiers who fought in Iraq. After all, they went in and were used as tools of war based on a now well-known lie from the President, Vice President, and many of their colleagues. They were forced to fight for a cause they might not have all truly believed in and the US was never in danger from Iraq. The job of the soldier in the military is to protect America, and its way of life, not earn a profit for corporations and other people, nor to fight in Iraq that had nothing to do with the 9/11 attacks on the United States to begin with.

For that, some payment to help for the loss of a dear family member, or the loss of limbs, or the many mental issues should be paid to those that have given up so much fighting for what has been proven to be a really, really, bad and intentional lie.

Next, to be kind - prison time should be served by those that instigated the war, actually a bullet to the brain, for war crimes should be the sentence for these lying politicians instead of the financial entitlements that they are now receiving. That includes those in the Bush Administration who instigated the war and mobilized the military illegally and those that profited the most from it.

Realistically, most of the blood is on their hands and their karma. They should be made an example of ... to show that we as American citizens will not stand for having our resources, and our soldiers and our tax money pay just to line the pockets of the already rich politicians. Politicians who act as mafiosa, and who see us as little more than tax-money resources and collateral. *In my humble opinion – A Bullet to the Brain will suffice. the editor.*

It's time we prove to the Government that this nation and the course it follows is made by the decisions of the American People and not greedy Military Capitalists.

Part 2: Jihad - The Extremist Tool of Control by Terrorism

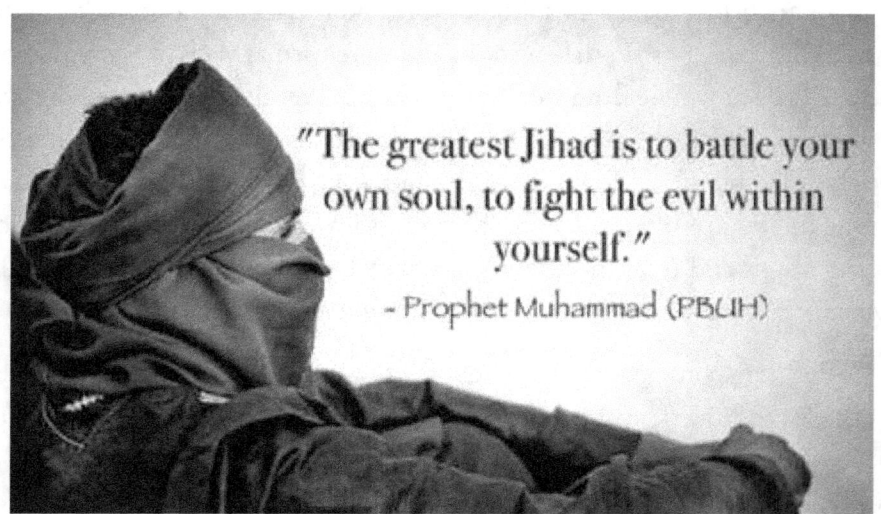

"The greatest Jihad is to battle your own soul, to fight the evil within yourself."

- Prophet Muhammad (PBUH)

There has never been such a threat to the existence of people that has taken hold of people's fears since the fall of Communism and has cowered nations to its unrelenting force, forcing them to prepare to fight against it both economically, and militarily. Of course, we're discussing the ramifications of Extreme Fundamentalism in Islam, and the threat of a global Jihad. Hell, even fear of the word itself.

Communism used to be the global enemy of those from the Western World and how it divided the world into Eastern and Western blocs. Most fearing a sort of attack from the Soviet Union, or one of its satellite states, like Cuba, or rising through Latin America and invading the US through Texas, and on up to Canada. We were scared of the spread of its influence from behind the iron curtain. However, since the fall of Communism in 1991, and the end of the Cold War, a new threat has arisen from the turmoil of the Middle East, and we are responsible for that, and it's more deadly and more effective at spreading its own influence than any other ideology in modern times.

However, the word "Jihad" used to have different meanings throughout its long history, and in a lot of ways started off as a bit more ambivalent than it currently meanings. Contextually, Jihad simply means "Struggle" or "Resisting," which in its original incarnation was a way to convey a way for the early Muslims to maintain the religion, and not as a call to war. In fact, any number of things could have a Jihad called on it, and a lot of them sometimes benign. You could have a Jihad called against things such as pork or bacon because the meat was viewed as unclean *(just as the Hebrews claim it to be – the editor)*.

You could have a Jihad against alcohol because alcohol loosened inhibitions and spurned habitual unproductive behavior and lewdness and impurity. You could even have a Jihad called against different kind of crops to harvest because they required people to go against the faith to cultivate. Or, you might have a Jihad against a different way of thinking because it went against the teachings of Muhammad. In fact, one of the most well-known Jihads that have been called for was against any art depiction of the prophet Muhammad because Muslims believed that it gave rise to idolatry, believing that people would worship the image of Muhammad instead of the prophet himself. Again, idolatry is against the law of the Hebrews, their brothers, as well.

It's only been within the last century that the term Jihad has changed meanings. It went from peaceful, struggling against something (or conscious resistance) which went against the Muslim faith to becoming a term used as a battle cry for a so-called holy war. Yes, a Holy War to simply target and kill anything, or anyone that they do not agree with.

The question then becomes…Why? Why did it change all of a sudden, and how did it change? Islam as a religion has been around for centuries, if not outright a millennia. While it's never outright been a religion of peace as some moderates or liberals might claim, it's never truly been that different from Christianity as a whole. In fact, on the whole, it paces with

Christianity regarding size and how violent it's been in its history, despite Christianity being an older religion and all. While, for centuries, Islam has expanded, by sword and by book, it's never instigated terrorism against a group of people, simply expanding and allowing conquered people to either submit to it willingly or die.

In fact, even in some places they allowed the conquered to continue to practice their non-Muslim religion, but for a heavy tax. So, in a lot of places it became cheaper just to become Muslim even though the option to practice their own religion was there. But, it was cheaper to become Muslim.

Even at the time of the European Dark Ages, and well into the height of the Middle Ages, Islam was even seen as a beacon of progress, advancing mathematics, astrology, astronomy, medicine, pharmacy, and trade. While Roman Catholicism was busy saving what knowledge they could during the fall of the Roman Empire, Islam was advancing its knowledge from what it learned from the Byzantine Empire, and even expanding upon it.

So what happened then that changed everything? If from 900-1,500AD was considered such a golden age of Islam expansion, thought, and learning, despite the crusades and its various failures to expand into Europe. Why is it so different now? Why is it such a bastion of extremist hatred that creates a culture of suppression, blood, and violence, to the point that the whole of the Middle East has been steeped in blood and is considered the bloodiest area of the world today? Yes, the Middle East is the only place on earth that threatens the entirety of planet Earth and its people.

Things truly didn't seem to change all that much since the 1970's. However, before-hand several factors come into play. Most noticeably was first the fall of the Ottoman Empire. Without the influence of the Ottomans or any sort of sultanate, most areas of the Middle East splintered off into their own nations, separating themselves along ethnic, or nationalistic personalities and united that way.

However, things were actually, surprisingly looking up from that point in time. While the Middle East has never been peaceful by any stretch of the imagination, with the inclusion of oil as a prized resource it was quickly becoming one of the richest regions in the world.

However, with a few exceptions, all of this changed seemingly in 1979 with the fall of the Pahlavi Dynasty and the Iranian regime when various different factions within Iran sought to overthrow Mohammad Reza Shah Pahlavi, and instead set up an Iranian Republic led by Grand Ayatollah Ruhollah Khomeini. Since then, a wave of fundamentalism took hold of the region and set up a domino effect across the region.

While the Middle East was developing and becoming more westernized and progressive, many there felt that was a threat to Islamic culture and reversed it by instigating a call back to earlier times by bringing back Islam first and foremost as the religion of choice, not a religion of peace. With that, they quickly put to death any liberals or moderates who disagreed with them.

Since then, it's only become progressively worse.

The question becomes then: How do we fight them, and revert Islam to a state that it was a not long ago? If we cannot revert it, and exorcise the extremism from the religion as a whole, can we contain it and can we at least protect the victims from their hatred? There are a lot of answers for how to fight the extreme fundamentalism that has taken a hold of Islam, and a lot of them range from between too soft, or too harsh. However, it is the harsh answers that need to be in place and are in need of having to be enacted.

For too long the world has been held hostage by the extreme of Islam. Taliban, ISIS, Al Qaeda, Boko Haram, and many others that teach Islamic faith by the sword and through terror. These need to be dealt with in a systematic way that limits their ability to deal damage to the world at large and needs to be contained, nay eliminated, for the good of the world.

One of the first things that needs to be done is to not allow the extremism to expand and to be cut off at its sources, resources, and not allowed to be further instigated anywhere else. By cutting off the head of the serpent itself, you limit its ability to grow as a unified system. Indeed, we're seeing this even now in several major Fundamentalist groups whose leadership have been targeted and eliminated, and thereby creating enough infighting causing the organizations to splinter, and form different factions while turning on one another. This is something that needs to be continued and expanded, since if we target their leaders and kill off their warlords who claim to be holy men, then they'll have no one to rally behind. True, we run the risk of making them martyrs for their cause, but in the end a martyr is just an idea. Martyrs don't fund organizations, they don't plan attacks, and they certainly don't train new soldiers or give orders. They become an archetype, nothing more, nothing less.

Once they've fought among themselves, and various different factions have formed, their power becomes weakened, leaving them open to retaliation by a Coalition of nations intent on wiping out extremism once and for all.

It can even go even further than that by eliminating their funding sources, and then instigating a No Fly rule from anyone that leaves that part of the world, and also patrol the borders to keep extremists from crossing them and getting into other nations where they can enact terrorist plots. True, you run the risk of innocent people dying and being turned away. But, with no aid coming to those terrorist organizations that control their lives, the people will have no choice but to do one of two things. They could continue to submit, and wither away, or rise up and take control of their own culture, and tell the world that they won't stand for extreme Jihadis and the terror that they sow.

It's high-time that the citizens of those nations stop proclaiming that they don't support the extremists while keeping their back turned to their atrocities. By not allowing anyone from that region to leave at all, and no aid going in save the bare necessities for each man, woman, and child, you can them allow them to kill each other and let Allah sort them out in the end.

If that does not work? Perhaps the best course of action then is to simply take control of their holy sites and allow only those that conform to the non-extreme views of Islam in to practice their religion. By only allowing those that the world itself can come to accept, you not only cut-off access to the one thing the extremists feel is a connection to that culture that they've tried to ruin. But, only give access of the mosques to those that the world has come to accept instead. The moderates, the peaceful ones, the liberals, and even those that are conservatives, only just wishing to live their lives in calm, peaceful harmony. No blades, no guns, no bloodshed, and no violence allowed of course.

Worst case scenario, and one option just as extreme as the militants, is to be enacted against, is to simply kill them all and make it illegal to practice any form of extreme fundamental Islam, or be a part of any sect that preaches violence over peace. It's an extreme measure, but necessary to ensure the safety of the rest of the world and to keep the Terrorists from reaching all corners of the world to anyone else in any other nation. We all remember, of course, the acts that had been perpetuated in the name of Islam and how they've been stretched to all corners of the globe. Many Jihads were blood baths, again, because people lived in a pathway where Muslins wanted to walk through, instead of walk around, on their way to Hajj.

In 1915, Turkish Muslims declared a Jihad against Armenian Christians and killed 1,500,000 of them without any justifiable reason and now deny it even though photographic evidence exists. This is like the skinheads saying the Holocaust never occurred.

This year a Texas community center was shot up because they hosted a cartooning contest over the Prophet Muhammad. Charlie Hebdo, in France, was terrorized because it publicized works of art making fun of extremism, and many more incidents such as those have occurred around the world, mostly without justifiable cause.

It's time that an eye-for-an-eye should be enacted. For every attack that kills innocents, they'll must be struck in turn and wiped out, with a Bullet to the Brain, 'til the people rise up and retaliate against their oppressors, much as the Arab Spring's promises should have brought about. Who knows? It might also allow some stability to return to the region after a trial through fire and blood. One more pang of war, and then it can rejoin the rest of the world in becoming modernized and peaceful once again and have the freedom to worship as they wish without being told how to do so by some Islamic Mafioso.

Whatever the cost, something major needs to be done. Unlike other Dark Ages that have hit areas of the world in various times in human history, the infighting and anger stretches far beyond its region and has stretched beyond national borders, and ethnic lines. Truly the whole of the Middle East holds the world in a grip of terrorism, where people fear that death could come at any moment, simply because they happen to be residents in a part of the world that's angered someone, somewhere, far away. Children no longer fear the boogeyman and instead fear those whose ideals they cannot comprehend and wonder why those people in black clothing hate them.

Truly, we live in a horrific time, and something needs to be done about it as a whole, and every nation that does not stand for it should rise up together to end it.

Part 3: Remedies – The Proper Way to Deal with Terrorists.

Everyone agrees: Terrorists are bad people. It doesn't matter what flavor of terrorism that they come in, terrorists are bad people. They can be extremist Muslim Jihadist's intent on blowing up monuments or walking into a crowd to explode themselves and sow terror and chaos wherever they go. They might be homegrown militants who are tired of the government and are squarely anti-authorities who choose to stockpile weapons with the intent of using them.

Terrorists might even be hermits and loners who close themselves off in the woods in a makeshift shed with little to no electricity, just making bombs and with evil intent mail them to people. One might even just be a psycho with a gun, or knife, who feels he needs some form of vindication and doesn't have any real message except to shoot people in a mall because he can. At the end of it all, a terrorist is someone who incites chaos and fear into the hearts of people who would otherwise only want to go about having a normal life, or just enjoy a normal day.

The problem then, becomes, after they've been captured -- what the heck to do with them? What is the proper way to handle a terrorist? Sadly, there is no definite answer that can be determined on how to deal with them. All terrorists are cut from the same cloth, whether a foreign power trained them to be used against military forces as well as civilians, or they're domestic and go after people who share their citizenship.

The answer for those that are domestic, homegrown, United States citizens are caught by the police. This is relatively easy, given that we have a system of law in place for such a thing. Once captured, they go to trial, are told their rights, and if they've been found to be guilty of their crimes, sentenced to death. That's exactly what was done with both Timothy McVeigh and Terry Nichols and the Oklahoma City bombings when they blew up the Alfred P. Murrah Federal Building on April 19th, 1995. They went to trial, and Timothy McVeigh was found guilty and sentenced to death, where he was executed by lethal injection on June 11, 2001.

Foreign terrorists are different, though. Technically, all terrorists that are captured are considered enemy combatants and aren't afforded any rights by the United States Government, and so aren't expected to be treated the same as US citizens. However, therein lies the problem. When they're considered enemy combatants, and detained without release you're creating a deadly precedent. It's been shown time and time again that Government organizations are willing to abuse that stance to do what they wish.

Under Republican administrations, torture was often performed with the intent to extract information, and often times the lines between enemy terrorist, and civilian innocents became blurred. Who can forget, after all, Abu Ghraib and Guantanamo Bay? What needs to be done isn't easy, but is vitally necessary.

For starters, the United States needs to stop detaining enemy combatants and terrorists in detainment camps on foreign lands. One of those in Iraq was the breeding ground of ISIS. Because of that, it becomes a technicality that all of those detained in foreign prisons do not get the same standards or rights as domestic terrorists. The reason, who's going to check up on them overseas? Look at the torture techniques from Guantanamo. Not only that, but the laws of the United States only extends to military installations inside of the borders, and only the Federal Government has power there. Not only is this wrong, but it allows the US Government and the military to do as it pleases with them. Often they are housed in the open air exposing them to the elements with no privacy, waterboarding them, parading them around nude while beating them, and giving them little more than a blanket for the ground they sleep on, and a bucket to use instead of a bathroom.

Not only that, but it's common knowledge as well that extensive torture goes on there, even if it is called "enhanced interrogation." The form of tortures that they perpetuate on the terrorists in these encampments and detention centers range from "water-boarding" where the victim is placed on their back, a rag put over their face, and water poured over them to simulate drowning. Techniques like sleep deprivation, noise overload, withholding food, exposure to the elements, making them walk in front of others nude while beating them while walking, and other forms of humiliation and degradation all go into effect and are well-documented. Is that how Americans treat other humans.

There are a multitude of different things that can be done when detaining terrorists that need to change for the better. For starters, the United States needs to stop detaining these terrorists on foreign soils and instead ship them to the United States where they can be housed in specialized military installations where other government oversight committees can view them and make sure that they're at least being taken care at the barest minimum requirements. Torture as well needs to stop as it's been proven, repeatedly, that torture is not a useful tool when extracting information as terrorists under duress. They will simply lie to stop the pain and torture, and say anything just for it all to stop.

By doing this, the United States won't have to lose the moral high ground when it comes to fighting a war, and can again become a beacon of freedom, righteousness and compassion instead of merely being propaganda tools to inspire the citizenry.

By giving, at least, some modicum of respect to terrorists after detaining, they might even be broken of their ideology of hatred and be given a chance to at least make some restitution for their deeds. Plus, with all of that and a fair trial, they might even be proven guilty through the court system. And once convicted – they simply get a Bullet to the Brain.

Since, there has been several incidents where the United States has been wrong, and wrongly detained innocent civilians from the Middle East, claiming they were terrorists when they were nothing more than in the wrong place at the wrong time, it won't be easy. But, at least it'll improve the United States standing among the world, once more, instead of being viewed as an imperialistic juggernaut of military might.

One last thing, the author, is a strong believer in medical, psychological, and chemical technology and believes torture is unnecessary with the use of sodium pentothal, lie detectors, voice stress analyzers, and deep-level hypnosis (mind control) to get to the truth. In that way, no torture is needed, and true terrorists can be expedited to the bullet executioner.

Part 4: The Majority of our Congressmen Need a Bullet in the Brain

"If you think it's too expensive to take care of veterans,
then don't send them to war."

– Sen. Bernie Sanders (I-Vt.)

Soldiers throughout America's history have always been viewed with some sort of mixture of awe, reverence, and respect. Just like their counterparts throughout history, and in other cultures, and in other empires and nations. It's always been viewed that anyone who was willing to put aside their lives of comfort and ease to pick up the warrior's mantle to protect their nation should be treated with respect and admiration. For it is the sacrifice of their bodies and souls that the nation is protected from the enemies seeking to exploit it; American soldiers are no different.

The revolutionaries of the past are treated with the utmost respect even today, their bones have paved the foundations of the Republic after freeing themselves from the tyranny of the Monarchy in 1776. Those who fought in the Civil War during the time of conflict are romanticized by the living today, both Confederate and Union soldiers alike, through stories and ballads. These memories are told to us through the lens of history as if it was a storyboard conflict, replayed through historical re-enactors, movies, and even songsters.

Those brave souls who fought against the Axis powers of the 1940's are considered part of a generation known today as "The Greatest Generation" due to the untold number of deaths and destruction that they had to wade through on two fronts, in the Pacific and on the fields of Europe. Even Vietnam veterans, wrongfully maligned in their time, are seen today as victims of a wayward nation and treated with respect for the hell that they've been put through.

Through all of American History, veterans of all branches of the military have been treated respectfully and in the past have been taken care of for the choices that they've been forced to make.

The veterans of the recent Middle Eastern campaigns should be treated no differently than any others. After all, in no other time in American history since WWII, or even the Revolutionary War have Americans seen a resurgence of blind patriotism and awe of the American soldier. In 2003, we were coming off of nearly 2 years of the aftermath of the 9/11 tragedy that saw the United States under attack from terrorist forces from across the sea. We were told that these enemies hated us for our power and our way of life. We were fed the usual rhetoric by all of those within the United States political system.

Congressmen toeing party lines, war hawks of all stripes and feathers in lockstep as they, together with the President of the United States, rattled their sabers that we needed to go after those that were responsible. All this occurred while saying that they hailed from the Middle East, and the destruction of the Twin Towers and the attack on the Pentagon was a declaration of war, and NATO itself would respond to the attack swiftly, and without mercy.

Who, back then, could disagree with such sentiments? We saw the worst terror attack on U.S soil since the sneak attack on Pearl Harbor, on December 7, 1941, by the Japanese. We also saw an attack that was against our civilian population in the center of the greatest city in the world. Anyone who disagreed that we should go to war was branded as a traitor and a non-patriot to the United States. His opinions didn't matter at any rate.

The sentiment of the American citizens saw a resurgence of flags being waved, and a huge spike in military recruitment from everyone. High schoolers, National Guardsmen, and even celebrities wanted revenge for the attack. They all signed up to do their part, and were promptly given a pair of boots, and were told where to go, and who our enemies were and one primary objective … "kill them."

Things were going rather well in the Middle Eastern campaigns shortly after they began, despite the President circumventing Congress to get approval, and sending us to kill people in the wrong country. Many citizens warned of the dangers of going to war too soon. However, revengeful American gung-ho senses, and a need to avenge the fallen won out. From our learning the lessons of Desert Storm, the American military soon toppled not only the Taliban of Afghanistan but also Saddam Hussein's Regime in Iraq, even though he had nothing at all to do with 9/11. The Americans believed, whole-heartedly, in the lies of Weapons of Mass Destruction, and the rhetoric that was being brought to the table by Chaney's cronies to bring those responsible to justice, even though there was no evidence, and those charged with the war crimes were not at all involved or guilty.

Still, all seemed well with Osama Bin Laden taking to flight and gone into hiding, the trial of Saddam Hussein commencing, and all of it culminating with President George W. Bush on the deck of an Aircraft Carrier, giving a speech. Additionally, our soldiers were at the height of their popularity, many people giving thanks for their services, and viewing them as heroes. Many, listening to the tales of military bravery in impossible situations, up against all odds and against an enemy who hated them.

However, soon things took a quick turn for the worse for those in uniform, and problems started to arise and become apparent. While the military establishment had a good plan of attack, and could maneuver across the battlefield and beat down any enemy that stood up against them, what they didn't consider at the time was a good working exit strategy.

They simply thought if they conquered, established a pro-democratic, and pro-American government in the area, they could leave rather quickly. They didn't have a clue that they were battling an enemy whose tactics simply changed to guerrilla tactics, forcing the military to fight a battle of attrition. It started to become quite clear that the United States did not have the manpower to stay in the fight for the length of time needed.

Also, considering that after the Middle East campaigns started to turn into a meat grinder shortly after we achieved the so-called "victory," military recruitment slowly started to dry up as well. This resulted in plenty of fighting soldiers who were waiting to be rotated out or were signed up for multiple tours of duty after changing their minds. What should have been two tours at maximum for a single soldier became three, four, five, and sometimes upwards of seven tours in both Iraq and Afghanistan.

Also, soldiers suffered a lack of equipment, as well, having to purchase body armor, and sometimes ammunition with their hard earned money, instead of having it supplied by the United States military. Can you imagine that?

The most damning of all problems that our men in uniform faced, however, was the dwindling of benefits once they left the service and returned home, trying to adjust back to civilian life.

Returning home from battle, and leaving their battalions, they were promised benefits and rewards for their services. The government had made promises to take care of them. Health Benefits from the Veterans Affair hospitals. Therapy, both physical and mental for their battle scars that we can see, and those we cannot see (PTSD). Help with colleges for those seeking higher education once they returned from conflict zones, and more were promised. This included: help with housing, taxes, all for giving up at least 4 years of their lives to fight a battle that they did not ask for, and ultimately in defense of people who did not appreciate their efforts.

The U.S. government promised that if they fought for the American People, the American People would turn around and take care of them. Instead, what they ended up getting was practically a slap in the face for having faithfully served in the dusty fields of the Middle East. Returning home, they suffered indignity after indignity in the name of caring for them. The indignity was called DENIAL.

Of course, politicians used the military, through their own rhetoric and party lines, proclaiming the opposition did not care for the Warriors' well-being. But, Congress would use them as a shield to protect Congress itself from criticism, while claiming they were above reproach simply because they invoked the name of the military.

Congress uses them as political pawns, offering them handshake with one hand, with the other unseen hand stabbing them in the back, by denying them benefits, or decreasing their funding that they were previously promised for service.

Instead, Congress votes themselves pay raises (for doing nothing useful for their constituents), or giving a huge payoff to a military contractor in the private sector.

Facing not only dwindling funds for the Veterans Administration, veterans must contend with the knowledge that a growing number of the veteran population in America has died waiting for emergency medical care, or become homeless, and having considerable financial troubles.

As of 2014, roughly 33% of the homeless population were comprised of ex-soldiers, meaning that of the 23 million veterans living now as civilians, too many are living on the streets or in shelters. A surprising percentage that Congressional politicians love to point that out as a problem, but do nothing about. Instead, they just blame political opponents for not caring enough, when it is them, themselves, who don't care.

Not only that but while soldiers were willing to fight and die overseas, on their native soils a looming bureaucracy made it nearly impossible for those very same Veterans to even receive the aid that they needed and were promised to begin with. This has resulted in a massive waiting list that not only did not prioritize veterans based on who needs what more than others, but it becomes a "first come, first served" mentality that only respects those who get in line early.

On average, when a veteran goes to make a claim to receive some promised benefits, or receive the help they need, it takes roughly almost 300 days to process, almost a whole year before they start to see any benefits whatsoever. Even then, there's no back pay whatsoever. And this often results in homelessness as mentioned earlier. Veterans have been known to die while on this damned waiting list due to medical issues that they need help with. Some deaths result from injuries or diseases they have suffered during their tour of duty.

That's the least of what Veterans have faced. I've mentioned, Congressional politicians voted themselves a pay raise, and have also increased funding for the Middle East wars and Military contractors profiteering, appropriating funds to the rebuilding of both Iraq and Afghanistan, while simultaneously making additional budget cuts to the Veteran benefits. In 2015, the Republican Congress, the same Republicans who constantly run the narrative as the party who is supportive of the veterans and who care more about the soldiers, rhetorically lambasted anyone who dares speak against the veterans at all -- slashed more than $1.4 billion in veteran funding from the 2016 bill. This happened even after President Obama promised additional funding to rectify the problems of the past.

Instead of debating and coming to a compromise on the bill to make it fair for all of those who are in need, because the Government sent them to war, Congress instead played their usual political games of cat and mouse. Republicans refuse to discuss the issue unless the Democrats gave into their demands (thus nullifying any discussion), and the Democrats refused amendments to the bill unless the Republicans acknowledged the bill in its original form (thus nullifying discussion). All in all, Congress got what it wanted, a pay raise, while blaming each other's political party for the situation, and the Veterans of America lost again with no voice in this situation.

All in all, this is something that cannot continue to be tolerated. As the opening quote of the chapter has stated from Senator Bernie Sanders, the government continues to deny to work with the veterans to help them with the help they need. Simultaneously they increase the defense budget spending and rattle their sabers at other nations they are hostile towards, including North Korea, Iran, and other places, while simultaneously sending military aid to Libya, Syria, and other nations still affected by the Arab Extremism. And that's an issue that's not sustainable at all.

Opinions, however, might differ on how to go about rectifying this problem, but one thing is for certain, and that is that those in Congress need to change the way they work, especially when it comes to the military and it involves giving the veterans what they promised. Because of the problems that Congress has caused, military recruitment is at its lowest since the draft was abolished. The use of stop-loss tactics in bringing soldiers back into service and extending the contracts they sign when joining the military has done little to change that, even when lowering the requirements to join the military by allowing in non-violent felons to join the military as well.

Today, no one wants to join the military, be shipped off somewhere far away, and forced to fight an enemy that we should not be fighting with to begin with. Nor, should anyone be forced into serving tour after tour after tour, and then left with nothing once they are honorably discharged. All of this is more proof why Congress itself only has an 11% approval rating as of the time of this writing.

Each congressman, instead, must be called before the American people and made an example of. No longer should they be allowed to invoke the military as their shield of protection, claiming that their opinions and actions benefit the military and that they stand with the soldiers while they, in truth, only cut veterans benefits just to spite their political opponents.

For every pay raise that Congress gives themselves, double that should be invested, instead, into Veterans benefits to give Veterans the proper care that they need. So, if they vote themselves a 5% raise, 10% must be increased of the Veterans Affairs' budget. That way if they want to allocate the budget they have to make sacrifices elsewhere, such as the defense budget, or their own paychecks to pay for it. And, if they don't, instead voting against it they should be ran out of office, and made an example of, because, in the end, they're betraying the American people. But Congress was also spitting in the face of every soldier who has stood up for this nation, and continued in the proud tradition of everyone in the military that came before them, all the way back to the revolutionary war when this nation was founded.

And in the end, that is not right. Our soldiers deserve so much better than that.

CHAPTER III

Terrorism on the Home Front

Part 1: Keep the Police Honest

There is a disease that seems to be running rampant in the minds of the Police Force in the US, not only with the tools that are designed to protect us but also they've recently been armed to the teeth when it comes to wielding the tools that mean to seek our death. It's no secret that out of all the police forces seen around the world, that the United States police force is one of the most heavily armed, and widely varied regarding how to use the military grade equipment it has now received. In fact, it's no secret that since the 80's that our Police Force is slowly becoming militarized to the point of being indistinguishable from the US Military Forces that wield weapons of death.

In fact, it's also no secret that militarization of the Police Force has led to a lot of problems as well. Now, it seems if you read the news that the old motto of "Serve and Protect" has been replaced with the motto of "Shoot First, Ask Questions Later." Our news broadcasts are replete with views and news stories of the police abusing their powers, most of it at the cost of our lives. Who can forget the growing movement of "All Lives Matter" that is starting to crop up as a response to what the police have done when handling suspects.

Baltimore recently was in the news as the police bungled handling a suspect who was innocent of a crime and killed him while violently transporting him. Who can forget Ferguson where an unarmed teenager came at a police officer as the officer shot him several times, once in the head? Who can forget the time in California when six police officers hogtied a homeless man with mental issues and beat him to death as he screamed for his father to save him. Human lives don't even seem to matter when it comes to many police officers, and that extends even more so to the animal kingdom within the last year.

Recently, we read news about police officers killing beloved family pets. Yes, there's been a story in the news of an incident where a police officer became suspicious of a home invasion, went to check on in the hopes catching the thief red-handed. Instead, he came upon the family dog barking at him. Instead of assuming no thieves were there, he shot the dog and left. Believe it or not, the city later billed the family for the mess that the Officer caused.

The horrible part is that's not an isolated incident. In fact, there are videos on Youtube regarding police brutality when it comes to dogs. Most of them end in the poor animals' deaths as the police fire at them because they assumed the pets were becoming "too aggressive".

One video showed a canine companion barely out of his puppy stages being shot and killed simply for barking at police officers who stopped to question his owner after scuffing one officer's shoes. If they can show such callous disregard for animal lives why should we trust them to protect human lives? We shouldn't!

The worst part is you can't even blame training for this issue in a lot of situations, although you can blame lack of training. In huge, sprawling cities of the United States you can find academies that take in young hopefuls looking to enter into the police forces. In cities such as Los Angeles, San Diego, Washington D.C, New York, and elsewhere there are academies that train police potentials in how to arm themselves with the tools of the trade. Training also includes how to deal with suspects, the laws behind interrogation, how to detain, and even the law behind the actions of what they can and cannot do.

All well and good when they pass the exams and enter into the force, fully armed with the knowledge of how to act, but they can never truly squash the human element that loves the power behind the badge and the cunning to circumvent laws to bully the populace, or use force to their advantage.

Of course, that's just in large sprawling metropolises. In a lot of smaller towns in the United States, joining the police force takes little more than an afternoon's class on brushing up on the Constitution, and learning how to detain a suspect and read them their rights. If you don't fall asleep after listening to all this propaganda for three hours, you take an exam and if you do "good enough", you receive your badge, and a gun, and a uniform.

The only real difference is that in the police academies in bigger cities, you join the police after training and graduating and it becomes part of the structure of that given metropolis. But, with smaller communities, you really can be a police officer just by being friends with the police chief, or even having the mayor as your best bud.

All of these problems seemingly continue to crop up that leads to the question: How can we protect ourselves from the Police? Sadly, a lot of solutions that are viable are also not exactly lax when it comes to being issued. This is after all not a two-sided problem. There is no other side of the coin when it comes to citizens' lives. For starters, the first thing that can be done is after a shooting has occurred, you take the badge and gun of the officer in question, and detain him on criminal charges as well.

There are a lot of ways that an officer can take down a suspect without killing them, and only in the direst of circumstances should a gun ever be fired. By criminalizing it, you show that you mean business when it comes to protecting lives first, rather than letting death of an innocent person be the first answer. Plus, it shows that you have confidence in the police that are still around to take it seriously.

After all, out of all the human deaths that have happened when it comes to police killing suspects, most of them resulted in acquittals, and almost none have seen any jail time. If they don't comply with these new rulings and the police, continue to use violence as a first measure, then perhaps the best answer is to end their career, after they take a life, and simply a bullet to the brain as the answer for these murderous police themselves.

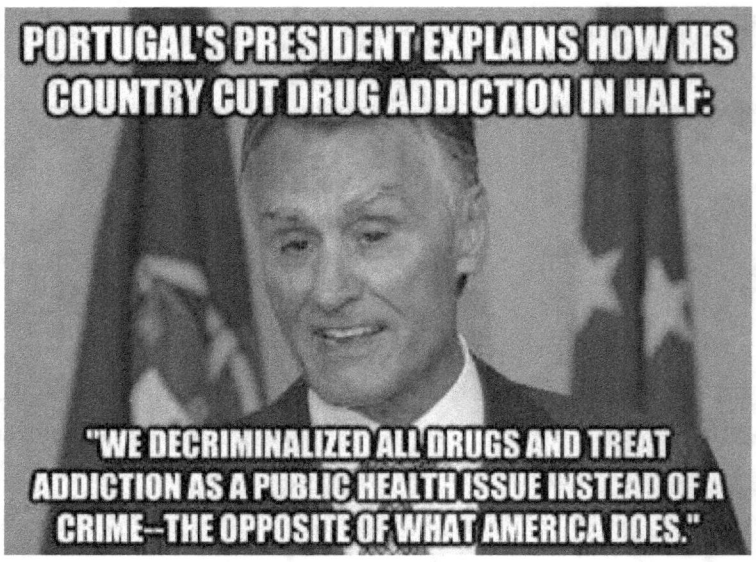

PORTUGAL'S PRESIDENT EXPLAINS HOW HIS COUNTRY CUT DRUG ADDICTION IN HALF:

"WE DECRIMINALIZED ALL DRUGS AND TREAT ADDICTION AS A PUBLIC HEALTH ISSUE INSTEAD OF A CRIME—THE OPPOSITE OF WHAT AMERICA DOES."

The History of Marijuana

History: Going back almost 5000 years, the Chinese Emperor Shen Neng, prescribed tea made from marijuana leaves for medicinal purposes including, malaria, rheumatism, gout, and other medical reasons. For the next 4000+ years, marijuana was popular in the Middle East and Asia, and along Africa's Gold Coast as a medicine. Certain Hindu groups considered marijuana for a stress treatment and also for use in religious ceremonies.

Old time doctors used to give patients marijuana for many problems including relief of pain, to suffering from earaches, and to help mothers during childbirth. In the late 1700's, the first medical journals in the United States suggested that hemp seeds and roots of the marijuana plant could be used for skin inflammation, sexually transmitted disease, and problems with incontinence.

Much research into the use of Medical Marijuana occurred as a result of Dr. William O'Shaughnessy, from Limerick in Ireland, who first learned about the use of marijuana medicinally while in India working as a medical doctor for the British East India Company in the early 1830's. While in India, O'Shaughnessy conducted experiments using marijuana on animals. Later, he began testing it on adult patients. He claimed it helped his patients with muscle spasms, rheumatism, nausea and vomiting, rabies, cholera, tetanus, diarrhea, and pain.

Soon medical doctors from the West were getting involved with a multitude of studies of the medicinal effects of marijuana. U.S. doctors hosted the first medical cannabis conference in 1863. Soon, U.S. and European Pharmaceutical firms had incentive to begin marketing various patent medications made from other substances to treat some of the same health issues that O'Shaughnessy used marijuana to treat. The first and foremost medication was Bayer's Aspirin, in the early 1860's.

There was something afoot at the end of the 1800's when it was realized that around 3-4% of the US population had become addicted to morphine which was an unlisted ingredient in several patent medicines. Medicines like – Dr. Fenner's Golden Relief. The country was in trouble due to the medical field not knowing what they were doing by using morphine in patent medicines. Then came the Pure Food and Drug Act in the earliest part of the 20th Century, which led to the FDA. Slightly earlier, a scientist at Bayer Pharmaceuticals discovered and trademarked "heroin" as a treatment for coughs and a substitute for morphine addiction. You can see the direction that this was going in.

Although none of this involved marijuana, it made distribution of opium-based and morphine-based products solely under medical doctors' supervision. People were arrested in drug stores for purchasing products they'd used for years for pain control. It was a complete shift in the American drug policy. In 1914, the Harrison Act made is a crime to use the medications, and through States' rights, the government taxed opium-based and coca-based medications. The tariff for drugs without paying the tax was imprisonment.

By the mid 1930's, 23 U.S. states had made marijuana illegal. Their reasoning was to put a halt to former morphine addicts through smoking marijuana. Plus, there was some prejudice against the new Mexican immigrants who often brought marijuana across the border with them. In 1937, the US Government had enacted the marijuana Tax Act, making marijuana illegal unless a tax was paid on it. Although the discovery and multiple medical uses of marijuana was realized, the government knew that they could not collect the tax because then users of it would be known to the government, therefore making its use illegal and punishable by imprisonment.

Grandma could no longer use marijuana for the treatment of her headaches and Grandpa could no longer use marijuana for the treatment of lumbago.

This resulted in great medical bills for treatment of symptoms that were treatable for less than 10 cents from herbs from the local drug store. Sometimes, the medical treatments resulted in poor choice of medications by doctors, unneeded surgeries by surgeons, and often death.

Let's move the clock forward to TODAY. Many countries are allowing usage and even the cultivation of cannabis by patients when needed for their medical issues. Again, proven by research, after previously proven by research, it is still controlled by the medical field and under prescription, the government is making it difficult for people needing medical marijuana to purchase it. In several countries and states where it's approved, the government seizes the herbal medication and persecutes those using it and legally selling it. Yet, with a prescription, medical marijuana can be bought it in several places in the world, or one in need might cultivate a small number of plants for their own use for treatment of their medical disorders.

However, during the period of marijuana being made illegal the following statistics have occurred:

Number of people arrested in 2013 in the U.S. on nonviolent drug charges: 1.5 million

Number of people arrested for a marijuana law violation in 2013: 693,482

Number of those charged with marijuana law violations who were arrested for possession only: 609,423 (88 percent)

Source URL: http://www.drugpolicy.org/drug-war-statistics

Enforcing marijuana prohibition costs taxpayers an estimated $10 billion annually and results in the arrest of more than 693,000 individuals per year -- far more than the total number of arrestees for all violent crimes combined, including murder, rape, robbery and aggravated assault.

Of those charged with marijuana violations, approximately 88 percent, about 609,000 Americans were charged with possession only.

Source URL: http://norml.org/aboutmarijuana

According to the United Nations, 158.8 million people around the world use marijuana—more than 3.8% of the planet's population.

Over 94 million people in the US have admitted using it at least once.

According to the 2007 National Survey on Drug Use and Health, 2.1 million people in the US abused marijuana for the first time that year.

Among 12- to 17-year-olds, 6.7% were current marijuana users in 2007.

According to US government estimates, domestic marijuana production has increased tenfold over the last twenty-five years: from 1,000 metric tons (2.2 million pounds) in 1981 to 10,000 metric tons (22 million pounds) in 2006. Not surprisingly, 58% of those aged 12 to 17 state that pot is easy to obtain. US marijuana users spent approximately $10.5 billion on the drug in the year 2000.

The latest numbers are out: nearly 800,000 Americans were arrested on marijuana charges in 2005.

According to the most recent figures available from the FBI, police arrested an estimated 786,545 people on marijuana charges in 2005 -- more than twice the number of Americans arrested just 12 years ago. Among those arrested, about 88 percent -- some 696,074 Americans -- were charged with possession only.

Source URL: http://www.alternet.org/story/47815/pot_prisoners_cost_ americans_$1_billion_a_year

That is 757,969 people arrested for crimes dealing with marijuana. Knowing how many people were arrested in 2011 for marijuana related offenses, let us calculate the cost of this incarceration for taxpayers.

According to Urban Institute Justice Policy Center, the yearly cost for an inmate in a minimum security prison is $21,006. Let us use this figure because 56% of all inmates are housed in minimum security institutions. According to the U.S. Sentencing Commission, in 2010, the average prison sentence for inmates incarcerated for marijuana abuses is 36.8 months.

With 757,969 individuals incarcerated for marijuana abuse, at $21,006 a pop, that is $15,921,896,814 to keep these individuals imprisoned for one year. At this rate, over the course of 36.8 months, $44,765,690,442 would have to be coughed up by the American taxpayer to clothe, shelter, offer medical, dental and psychiatric care, maintain, transport, and educate these individuals and maintain facilities for them to live in. This — $44 billion over more than 30 years — is the grand cost of petty crime.

Source URL: http://mic.com/articles/54803/this-is-how-much-marijuana-prohibition-costs-you-the-taxpayer

Nationally, according to the report, the marijuana arrest rate for African-Americans in 2010 was 716 per 100,000, while for Caucasians it was 192 per 100,000, meaning African-Americans were 3.7 times more likely to be arrested for marijuana possession.

Source URL: http://www.politifact.com/rhode-island/statements/2014/mar/16/naacp/new-england-naacp-says-african-americans-us-are-ar/

http://www.fbi.gov/about-us/cjis/ucr/crime-in-the-u.s/2012/crime-in-the-u.s.-2012/persons-arrested/persons-arrested

http://norml.org/aboutmarijuana/item/marijuana-decriminalization-talking-points-2

The United States is a close second only to Russia in its rate of incarceration per 100,000 people. In 2010, more than 746,000 people were arrested in the USA for marijuana-related offenses alone.

http://legalizationofmarijuana.com/

So, having read this – does any of this make sense to you. Spending 16 billion dollars per year to put people in jail for smoking Mother Nature, and it's a good medication for headaches, backaches, and cures a lot of illnesses. It's a great and safe recreational substance, far safer than alcohol. The world has gone absolutely crazy. And, in the process – the people who would benefit most, medically, from using it for their medical condition are deprived, abused, imprisoned, and made subject of police harassment and brutality. Welcome to the United States of America.

Part 3: Incarceration Nation – The Prison Industrial Complex & Modern Slave Labor

There's a current incarceration problem that the United States has, and nothing is being done to fix it. In fact, it's a problem that has grown exponentially within the last several decades, and neither lawmakers nor the citizens of the United States seem to care. Some view it as a good thing that shows how many people are currently in the prison system, locked away for their crimes and away from normal, everyday people who don't commit crimes at all. However, that only exacerbates the problem and creates a new one. Namely how the Prison system itself is incarcerating and its own systems are turning prisoners into cheap or slave labor, and prison management are profiting off of the backs of these prisoners.

Everyone can agree easily on a few points, though. Prisons are needed, and at times are useful. After all, they're designed to be a way to lock people away who would be a menace to everyone else in a community, and should be a place to not only punish people for crimes but as a place of rehabilitation as well. If someone performs a viscous, violent crime that results in a physical attack, sexual attack, or shows no remorse in taking advantage of people for personal gain, then they should be locked away for years as a form of restitution to their victims and punishment for breaking the law. But, they are not. They may be locked away – but there is no restitution. The problem though is that for the majority of people behind bars currently, the majority of them are for non-violent crimes that other developed countries around the world treat as a problem on a personal level as opposed to a societal one. Since the 1990's with the start of the "War on Drugs", minor offenses that include possession of marijuana have contributed to the rise of incarceration rates, with marijuana being a catalyst for nearly 80% of the increase in the number of inmates.

In fact, a first time drug offense usually carries a 5-10 year jail sentence, while in other developed countries the same drug sentence would be six months in jail, or a fine and mandatory rehab. It's gotten so bad that there are currently 2.4 million people behind bars, which means that 1 in every 150 citizens is arrested and lives in the prison system. What makes this even more staggering is the fact that the United States only has 5% of the current world population but houses 25% of the world's prisoner population. Hell, since the 1980's, the Prison population has more than quadrupled in size to the current levels that they are now.

The problem that this creates mostly is a huge Prison Industrial Complex, and under our current capitalist system, it has created a business (a hotel empire) that has become the for profit business of the future. The more people that are behind bars, the more money that is poured into the system making corporations that run prisons rich.

To put this into perspective, the United States has spent over $80 billion on incarcerating prisoners alone since 2010. That's a lot of money, sure, but the main problem with that is that most of it went to third party sources (corporations) that take on the bulk of the pressure to house the prisoners as a way of letting the Government cut costs.

This is how it works: A corporation builds the prison, houses inmates, and spends money training staff, paying the utilities and upkeep, guaranteeing all the monetary penalties that come with running a prison.

The United States in turn pays a stipend per year to the prison per prisoner housed. That money is to go towards paying for the housing, clothing, and food of that prisoner, and any money left over naturally goes as a profit to the Corporation itself. This equals big bucks for the Corporations housing the prisoners and is why a lot of times they restrict and maintain a tight hold on the prison population they oversee. After all, it's a place people go to be punished for murder, rape, embezzlement, and drug charges, and no one really cares about prisoner rights as long as they're off the street and people can feel safe. So, technically, prisoners don't have many of their rights since they were revoked by the Federal Government. Prisons, can, therefore, withhold a prisoner from release, and even be allowed to increase their prison sentences for any minor infraction within the prison itself, that can range from disorderly behavior to outright aggression.

The worst part of all of this 'for profit' business is that they are, literally, holding people prisoners creating a modern day caste of slaves, with much of them being made up of non-violent offenders who were charged with possession, and not even actual sales, of minor drugs. The Prisons that house them create modern day chain gangs by outsourcing prisoners as labor for anything from ditch digging to field work, to factory work. In fact, it has become such a clichéd image of prisoners stamping out license plates, or digging a ditch by the side of the road, even picking up litter all while chained up.

None of the prisoners are paid for this either, even when working in sweltering heat with no compensation for their work. In fact, there is compensation, but not to the prisoners. The private prison corporations get paid for the outsourced work to further increase their profits, claiming that it's a good thing and that the prisoners are being used for the betterment of society, neglecting to mention how they're being used as a slave labor force to further their own profits.

Naturally, this needs to be stopped for the betterment of society, and things need to change. For the most part, the business of for profit prisons to house prisoners needs to stop because it stops the problem it at its source, which is simply greed motivated. Instead, creating a non-profit framework, insures that the prisoners are being housed and are properly cared for without anyone pocketing money off of their backs.

The second problem comes from the population itself since the United States has seen one of the highest prisoner population in the world recently. What needs to be done is to eliminate minor drug offenses as felonies, and reclassify them as misdemeanors at best. Misdemeanors tend to carry lighter sentences, rarely ranging into years, as well as fines and mandatory rehab for their crimes. By decriminalizing non-violent crimes, prison populations would see a massive decline. Thus, running a prison for profit would become impossible and a fruitless endeavor.

In fact, criminalize those who design and run the for profit prison systems first, since under the law it constitutes slavery, especially when putting people to work against their will without compensation, and also for abusing prison inmates because that has become the norm.

CHAPTER IV
Robber Barons

Part 1: Citizen's United

There is a massive problem currently occurring on in the United States, under the Capitalistic system, which no one seems to be noticing, or caring about. It's causing the downfall of our great nation. It used to be that, under communism, we'd fear losing our homes to the state, our savings to other people, and be forced to labor eternally for little to no wages and that we wouldn't have a say in the government.

However, all of that has come to pass under Capitalism. Think about it today. When it comes to losing our homes, we fear that our homes would be foreclosed on by the banks when we cannot afford them anymore. Take out a mortgage to fix your home up or pay it off, and end up not paying and the bank will repossess it, even if you own the house. It's not yours, it is collateral for the bank. When it comes to our savings, we fear that we'll lose it, and rightfully so. Under Capitalism in the United States, we can very easily lose our savings if we're not properly insured for health care cost, and even then, insurance more or less is treated as something that you must have by law, which in practice is more or less extortion. You need health insurance for every visit to the doctor, with hour-long check-ups costing more than $750 in most cases, and minor surgery costing tens of thousands of dollars.

While insurance lessens the sting of payment, your insurance company can still deny your claims, increase your policy premium costs so you pay more, or outright drop your coverage on a whim if they feel you're a liability to their profits.

The system is rigged, that much is obvious. Look at all of the Presidential candidates of the last 4 election cycles. All of them very rich, all of them millionaires with very little of them being self-made in anyway, most of them coming from money or business and already having started life that way from family inheritance. Even congressmen in government are the same way. Doctors, Lawyers, Businessmen, all of them super rich.

When was the last time you heard of a plumber who sat on a table in government, when was the last time you had someone who came from the middle class, or even the lower middle class, rise up from the ranks to become successful and run for politics outside of a local level? I think that the last poor man to become President of the United States was Abraham Lincoln – that's how long ago.

No matter what, in the United States, your own voice won't be listened to. How often have politicians played their games, and the citizens responded to it, only to be ignored? The teachers strike in Wisconsin, several years ago, saw thousands of teachers from all over the United States stand in solidarity with one another to tell the Governor that they don't accept the loss of their union rights to strike, congregate, or having bargaining power. The net result: the state government went ahead with the Governor's political ambition to destroy their rights.

Look at the riots caused by the Occupy Wall Street movement of several years ago, and how they protested against Wall Street being involved in politics and accepting government bailout money despite their bad business practices which nearly caused the entire U.S. economy to collapse. No one else would have been "too big to fail" and given tax money collected by the citizens to fix their mistake, and the Occupy movement spread throughout the country to protest tax money being used for people who prey on their financial need.

Yet, the Occupy movement fell by the wayside, as no one took their claims seriously or even allowed them a chance. The same can be said of another political movement on the opposite end of the political spectrum with the Tea Party Movement, which initially formed as a response to call out politicians for their dirty deeds and actions, before devolving into liberal hate and President Obama opposition.

Even then, their initial voice was as a response to a problem that they saw arise in the United States' governing body. It was formed as a way to combat it before being shoved aside, shouted down, and shut out of any constructive feedback, forcing the fringe of the group to remain while the moderates got shoved aside.

To make things even worse, Corporations seemingly sprung up overnight to become the predominant voting power within the United States. Ever since the 2009 Supreme Court ruling titled "Citizens United", the Supreme Court's ruling stated that it would allow Corporations and Union spending to be uncapped, allowing them to spend theoretically unlimited amounts of money on political issues. Since then, Americans have debated it. In the end, this means that a Corporation, by the law, is treated as a person instead of a conglomeration. Because of that they can have a voting power, and as a voting power they can show their support with money. So now, because of that ruling, a Corporation has the same rights as any other citizen in the United States, but the problem becomes obvious when it shows that those Corporations have more rights than citizens do.

As a person without corporate backing, you have only a fairly small number of options to being heard. Obviously, you as a normal person cannot spend millions on a political candidate who you favor, and your vote essentially counts as 1.

Therefore, corporations already outclass a normal citizen by the fact that they have more capital to spend on the political system to be heard. And, realistically CORPORATIONS ARE NOT PEOPLE. However, most of these corporations do not have to pay taxes like citizens. They are arranged and incorporated to be tax-free entities.

Also, case in point, is the fact that a Corporation can deny its own employees health insurance, dental insurance, and any other insurance, and because it also has the right (as a person after all), to have freedom of religion. Therefore, a Corporation can squelch any other religion from anyone else that works for the corporation despite it being illegal for businesses to discriminate.

A corporation though doesn't pay nearly as much tax as a normal person does, and most of them that do impact elections are tax-free, and they have more voting power, more money, and more of a say in government.

Obviously, this is leading to a massive number of problems that are coming out with how Corporations are using their new found political power within the last 5 years to swing their weight around. The only way that this can be fought, and restore the balance in favor of the citizens of the United States is to revoke the ruling that the Supreme Court enacted in 2010. And then, treat Corporations as they are: multinational businesses made up of businessmen who should be, by law, limited in what they say or do in Government and taxed at the personal income tax rate.

Politics and Business should be separate for the good of the Nation.

Part 2: Chris Christie's Corruption

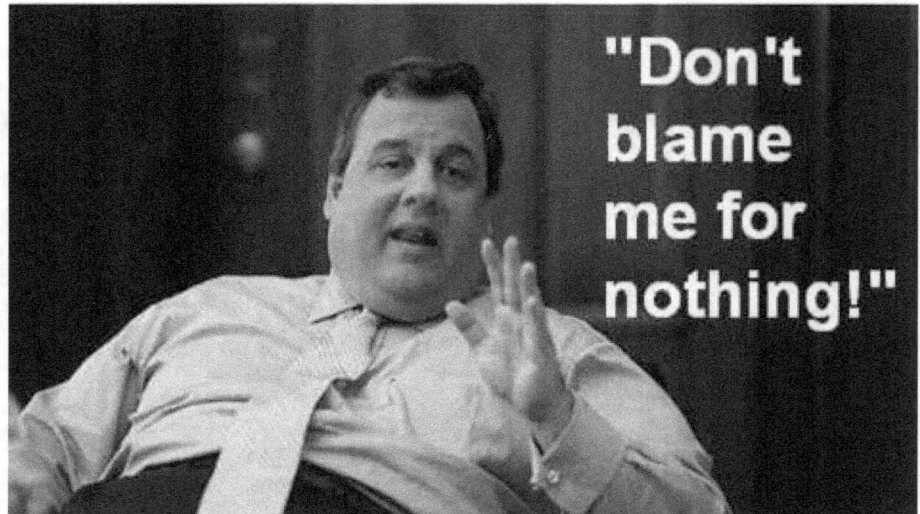

"Don't blame me for nothing!"

New Jersey has a reputation, among all of the states in the union, as one of the most corrupt places in the United States. And, that's no small feat when you consider it as it runs up against places such as Chicago, Illinois, and New York City, or even in places where you'd expect rampant corruption to be the norm such as Los Angeles, San Diego, Las Vegas, Hollywood, or Washington D.C.

So it comes as no surprise, whatsoever, that Bridgegate happened, or as it's more known as "The George Washington Bridge lane closure scandal." All of the problems regarding the George Washington Bridge lane closure happened in the fall of 2013, around September 13th. No one knows exactly the reasons why two lanes of the bridge were closed, choking traffic in a deadlock traffic jam that lasted for nearly three days. But, it should come as no surprise that in the May of 2015, three aides to NJ Governor and 2016 President hopeful Chris Christie were indicted on charges to commit conspiracy, one of which resulted in an arrest so far.

There's no exact explanation as to why two lanes were shut down. However, the prevailing theory that's been stated that Chris Christie used the closure as a retaliation against Fort Lee's Mayor, Mark Sokolich (D) for not endorsing Chris Christie in the 2013 gubernatorial election when Christie was running to become New Jersey's Governor again. In fact, this is the prevailing theory that was given as to why it was done and is even supported and alleged by Federal Prosecutors in May of 2015 against the three aides of Christie, with a guilty verdict against one of them. It makes it seem all the more likely that this is the reason behind the shut-down of the bridge.

Of course, another prevailing theory was because it was a possible negative effect on Mayor Marl Sokolich's endorsement of the "Hudson Lights" project, which was a $1 billion developmental project that was centered on the bridge, and along the waterway. Not only would the development had been a moot point should the bridge have been shut down, but would have cost even more money to continue development while the bridge was being delayed to reopen.

However, no matter what the true cause is, there's no denying that the effects were negative on Fort Lee. However, that was a retaliation used by Chris Christie against Mark Sokolich, which was not even helped when e-mails of the incident came up during the investigation that pointed to Sokolich as not playing ball with Chris Christie's camp, and using derogatory terms against him.

Of course, the most laughable part of this entire incident is how Chris Christie has gone on record, in February of 2014, on the Bridges Closure, a full 7 months after the event to claim he had no knowledge about the two lane closure at all. Frankly, of course, that smells of bullshit that he would have had no idea at all in the closing of the bridge. Because, not only did he have the three people working directly under him, those three just happened to conspire against someone else using tax payer funds, and the government's time to plot this out.

This sort of incident takes careful planning and a go ahead that those without political clout could not do without the approval of someone in a higher position. The worst part of it, of course, was when Chris Christie hired a law firm, "Gibson, Dunn, & Crutcher" to perform the investigation behind the whole thing in Chris Christie's name. This, of course, was a surprise because no one else in all of New Jersey knew about this plan. But, they were hired to clear Christie of any wrongdoing what so ever in the closure of the bridge. No one hires a law firm to do an investigation!

For starters, this too is bull and a possible stinks of corruption, as it's been alleged that no one within the law firm could interview any key participants or witnesses within Chris Christie's camp. Because of that, they could not have been able to evaluate the entire incident.

Without key testimony, plus the fact that they are a law firm of defense attorneys, and not a public prosecutorial team which is a right that belongs with the state or federal government, their word means nothing. Not only that but as others have even suggested it read more or less like a key defense that Governor Christie would more than likely use should criminal charges be levied against him in this scandal.

What does this all show? It demonstrates that political corruption runs deep and is still a problem in American politics. Especially, corruption is alive and well and living in bastions of New Jersey where it seems members of government can use their political weight to levy traffic, bridges, and other punishment against a political opponent they do not like, and can damage reputations, city development projects and never face any jail time. That's Republican justice. However, their aides beneath them certainly will after being thrown under the bus. If any good development came from all of this, it's that the polls among New Jersey citizens do not look upon the Governor with any sense of approval. Most, of course, believing him to not be honest at all, and that any good will he had developed in the last 4 years has practically vanished, no doubt ruining his bid for the presidential seat in 2016.

But, that does not go deep enough among some people with strong opinions regarding the incident. A lot of people believe that even if charges don't come against Chris Christie, he's shown that he's willing to damage political opponents, and throw his underlings under the bus, and, into the hands of the federal prosecutors when it conveniences him.

So even if he does not become impeached, the citizens of New Jersey should vote him out of office at their earliest convenience. And if that's not enough, New Jersey voters should also rescind his pension and any sort of government entitlements for him. That will send a strong statement to not only him, but any member of any state government, any Congress, or any other branch of the United State political machine, that corruption will not be tolerated.

And, even if there's a small whiff of possible corruption, that position should be weeded out and given to someone willing to use the position correctly for the good of its citizens, and not the good of their own political ego. Or maybe, Chris Christie just needs a Bullet in the Brain.

Part 3: The move towards mass privatization.

The rising costs that the United States has seen within the last 30 years in infrastructure that in past would never have been considered for privatization is now occurring. Things such as roadways, prisons, the Federal Reserve, and even schools have all been privatized and put in the hands of corporate management. These were once handled by the Government. It seems like an easy enough solution to a growing problem of lack of funds since after all it means that instead of the responsibility of maintaining and fixing belonging to the Federal Government, it now belongs in the hand of private interests.

However, it's not that simple and has presented a whole host of other issues affecting millions across the country. Put, in the wrong hands greed has led to major issues. Some include major disrepair to what was once a beautiful operational system. This disrepair caused by private corporate interests whose owners have become millionaires and billionaires at taxpayer expense.

How did a problem like this occur, though? Sadly the problem lies with the Government itself and how it's handled itself since the 1970's. It's no secret, especially since it's been a highlight of Presidential campaign rhetoric since the 90's that the United States has a huge spending problem. It chooses to spend money on things it can't really afford. They are choosing to spend money not only on defense purposes, but foreign aid, kickbacks, government employee's and benefits (huge entitlements), the military (more than 52% of the US budget), and anything else that benefits the government elected officials. All the while borrowing money from foreign powers (mostly China), and not repaying it. This is increasing our national debt by the billions each year. In fact, it's gotten to the point that most of the money spent that doesn't go to military purposes for defense as well as War gets rolled into paying back interest on what we owe instead of going towards other things such as schools, Hospitals, Infrastructure, Police, Firefighters, and more.

All to combat our national growing debt, of course, which barely leaves money for anything else. Because also the Government is highly unwilling to increase taxes, tantamount to political suicide to even suggest such a thing, no new taxes are levied to fight off the debt further or pay for the things we need. So, instead what the Government has done is privatize things instead thinking that operational costs will be cheaper.

That's become the solution. Slowly, over time, the Government has given up almost complete control over certain aspects that it had controlled in the past to private corporations. These corporations are willing to take on the monetary risk of controlling, running, and paying for certain parts of our society. They either charge for services or take a government stipend. While, for certain things, this has resulted in some services that have improved the quality of life, including National Parks, National Forests, Waterworks, Schools, etc. In other cases, it's created a whole new industry that's been fueled by greed, and the idea of profit off the backs of citizens.

Take for instance the increasing price of the Toll Roads as an example. First and foremost, private contractors were hired and paid to build super highways that connect major cities throughout the United States, and most people agree that with these super highways having been built it's allowed the shipping of goods across the country to arrive rather quickly. In fact if you started on the East Coast, you could end up at the West Coast in a little under 48 hours, which was a massive increase to other ways that were previously available.

However, the price of the tolls themselves have increased steadily, over time, to help offset the cost of the roads themselves. This means that for people who need to travel they need to cross country in a hurry, they need to pay their way to travel roughly every 30 or so miles or be forced off the highway to use local roads.

Of course, that's a minor nitpick in comparison to some. After all, you can still get off the highway and travel across other U.S. local roads that are all free to access without payment, you just must deal with no rest stops, no restaurants of any standard quality, police speed traps, and millions of potholes.

But, what happens when that idea of privatization comes to a societal construct that's desperately needed? We've already seen what happens when those same principals of profit touches upon the Prison system. After all, since the 90's and the criminalization of drug possession, prisons have seen an increase of their total prison population jump nearly to four times what it was nearly 40 years ago. In fact, the total prison population of the United States exceeds 2.5 million Americans, and affects mostly lower middle class to lower class people, and largely effects minorities in poverty stricken areas.

The United States spends upwards of $20 billion annually just to house them to various contracted companies throughout the United States, and there have even been scandals involving Judges taking kickbacks to send people to prisons or even detention centers.

Who can forget the "Kids for Cash" scandal of 2008 when Judge Mark Ciavarella and Senior Judge Michael Conahan took bribes from a For Profit children's detention center that was owned by Robert Mericle just to increase the number of residents inside the detention center so the owner could charge the Government more to house them.

Prisons and roadways are not the only institutions that have fallen victim to the problem of sacrificial privatization. Look at situations about the current problem of Police and Fire Fighters, two basic societal needs that's essential to keeping a community running smoothly, and from collapsing in on itself.

Because of the annual budget problem of the Police and Fire Fighters less money is available, and donations are drying up, worker's compensation and training has fallen upon private organizations that charge for the training, equipment, and everything to keep the Fire and Police institutions running. Sometimes these operations which require full-time staffing, have instead become part time. When profit and greed overtake common sense, we end up with the problems we have now where Police don't get the training they need to protect citizens. Their lack of training and lack of ethical standards result in Police shooting citizens in the street, sometimes for minor infractions, or sometimes by error. Firefighters are frequently becoming purely voluntary now without pay to compensate them.

This needs to change, and soon before our infrastructure and communities fall apart. What can we do to fix things and set it on the right path? Many things, actually. For starters, the US Government needs to man up. It needs to reach down where its balls are supposed to be and give them a yank to let them loose, and then realize that Government has gotten us itself into this mess, and Government needs to get us out of this mess – without privatization.

For starters, everyone needs to realize that yes, taxes suck. No one likes taxes, but the citizens must realize that for a small change in their taxes roads and bridges can get fixed, Cops will get properly trained, Fireman will get paid, prisons can operate properly and cost less, and people will be living normal free, and respectable lives. *And yes, Millionaires must pay their fair share, not 13% like Mitt Romney. Hell, he probably gives more to the Church. – the editor.*

What's to stop the Government from abusing that new found revenue? A Bullet to the Brain Theory – where they stop fighting unnecessary wars in the Middle East and stop creating new problems for the US. By creating a non-partisan oversight committee to properly oversee the allocation of money, the Government would see their investment start to bring us back to prosperity, instead sliding down into chaos, which is where we've been aiming since the 80's. Will the Government step up to do what is right? Only time will tell.

Part 4: Destroying Lives, for Profit.

"...corporations have been enthroned & an era of corruption in high places will follow..."

- Abraham Lincoln

Corporations have been around for a very long time. They are not a modern invention based under capitalism alone but have been around for centuries. At its base, Corporations are a group of investors gathered together to share resources, with each board member taking on equal responsibility for financial gain, selling stock to others as a form of investment, and equality in the sharing of the business's fortune, and overseen by one board member as the chairman.

In an ideal world, Corporations would simply exist for: Sharing the burden among like-minded investors to further an agenda and insuring that the company remains stable, and can function in the economy. However, it's easy for greed to take hold and the selfish pursuit of profit to become the number one priority of a corporation.

When this happens, it's not about appeasing a customer base, building a product or service that people would gladly pay for, or even creating a corporate atmosphere that would foster pride in the corporation. Instead, it becomes about maximizing how much money those at the top can attain, sacrificing and penny pinching from the top down and liquidating all assets that have no function to the pursuit of profitable gain.

Even worse, of course, is when that pursuit goes from the workplace to impact customers, creating an imbalance in the economy that hurts those who rely upon the corporation and its services for various reasons. Normally, for local, small businesses, this isn't much of a problem. It's sad and a painful lesson when a company's sole motivation is profit, but the market tends to balance out when competition opens up and offers the same thing at a better price, with better customer service.

Corporations though by their nature are large conglomerations, and typically those that survive to dominate an industry often become the sole supplier of those goods and services over a large territory, nudging out competition simply by force of monetization means alone, or through simply shutting down the competition through negative advertisements. At least that is a Republican theory and how they try to shut out the Democratic with negative advertisements.

The most dangerous part of this all, though, is that this greedy pursuit of profit can end up destroying people's lives. For some luxuries in life, such as the entertainment, restaurants, or other non-essentials you can simply cancel your account with the company, unplug your cable TV, not go out to eat and find another hobby to occupy your time. Television costs too much? Switch to either basic television or read a book. The price of beef has gone up as well? Switch to other sources of meat such as chicken, or pork, or become a vegan or vegetarian.

There are literally a million other options that one person can do for entertainment and some of them don't require money to enjoy. But, there are goods and services that are needed, that people cannot afford and through the pursuit of profit by corporations, can severely limit someone's health and happiness, or possibly destroy their lives.

Take, for example, a situation that caused the collapse of the housing market during the recession of 2008. The problem there was that occurred when a lot of major banking corporations were selling off mortgages and giving out bad loans to people with little to no credit score in the hopes of driving up the premiums for those people to return a massive amount of profit later. Naturally, many couldn't afford the higher monthly payments and defaulted.

Then, the Banks repossessed the homes because they were used as collateral. That maneuver created a situation where too many had a low credit rating from losing their homes through repossession and foreclosure. Plus, not enough buyers in a market at that time. Finally, the real estate market crashed.

Not only that, but we also had a derivative market that treated these mortgages as if they were a gamble, where companies would bid on (or gamble) on whether or not certain individuals would default. If they defaulted, the Banks made money, if they didn't default, the Banks still made money. Those who lost out on the gamble were those person who acquired the loan which the Banks knew would be defaulted on and those who got thrown out onto the streets as homeless when the whole economy bellied up.

Another example of this predatory profiteering is currently occurring is with college tuition and the rise of the "For Profit" colleges. Colleges all around the nation have increased their tuition, often tripling in cost, forcing students who want a good education at an accredited University to have to take out huge loans for their education. They often borrow at the same banks who screwed over home owners during the 2008-2010 recession. By taking out these loans out, and forcing students to repay over many years with interest colleges essentially enslaved the future of these students. Even a bankruptcy does not erase that debt, and new legislation is being considered that won't allow a person who owes student loans unemployment or Social Security benefits unless all of that debt has been paid off, baring death or massive physical injury that results in their becoming a cripple. Welcome to the United States of Slavery. Just so you know, in Cuba and Mexico, University tuitions is free.

Next, the Insurance Industry.

Of course, you have the problem of those who need insurance, and who pay a massive amount to have that coverage. Whether it be health insurance, life insurance, car insurance, home insurance, mortgage insurance, disability insurance, or anything else that would be a disaster and near impossible to recover from if something bad occurred.

A lot that can be said regarding the huge insurance scam that takes place now, as insurance companies have the sole right to deny you your claims. Even if you've paid for coverage for those situations, they simply claim insurance fraud or drop you if you become a big liability for them. Then, you'd have to hire a lawyer to fight the insurance companies, and don't get me started on lawyers befrauding their clients. It happens every day, and not only in the US. But, let me say, that basic liability insurance for automobiles in Mexico – is about $45 per year. Interesting ....

Horror stories abound from other industries in the current United States economy. Ranging from Prisons to Telecommunications, to the Minimum Wage, which is poverty level living, and others. It's gotten so bad that it's one of the major reasons that the last 30 years has seen the decline of the middle class and the rise of the poverty level worker.

There needs to be something done to prevent this scenario from further destroying the US and creating a much wider income gap than currently exists. Dragging predatory bankers and CEO's out to the street, with the 25 cent cost of a bullet, of course, is one option, proving that this sort of behavior should be made illegal.

Capitalism itself is a great system to live under. Freedom of choice to form businesses that compete with one another, and the freedom of choice on who to vote for. Still the Government needs to step in and create some form of oversight regulation that prevents unethical corporate attacks from happening to people. Forcing good, honest, hardworking Americans out of their homes, and onto the streets, with little to no insurance, and enslaving them to a lifetime of debt, is not what our founding fathers had in mind.

Part 5: America's Wars: Greed and Corruption Lining Pockets

There's a popular saying about war that's been evoked recently. They say that War never changes, often implying that War throughout the centuries has been relatively the same. Meaning, of course, people go out and kill each other, often in horrible ways.

From ancient times with sticks and stones, to the medieval era with blade, horse and steel, to more modern times where we kill each other with guns and explosives, often from a great distance from one another. It's true, War never changes, since if you get several people together and a reason to hate one another we'll find ways to murder one another if we go to war. However, there's a stark difference in modern times in the reasons we fight as opposed to the past.

In the past, when we went to war it was often for different reasons. Whether it was because we were fighting for territory, over religion, or because our neighbors looked and acted different, that was sufficient enough reason to go to war with them. Even in the United States we've gone to war for various reasons, some of which were justified in the end.

Take for example the first war that the United States fought. The one we were fighting for our independence in 1776. Most Americans know this from history, so there's no need for rehashing. But, at it's base this fledgling nation felt that it needed to secede from the British Empire for various reasons, and so it took up arms against the British Crown and declared its independence from the British Empire. With the help of different allies, America won its freedom and became the Nation we live in today.

Who can forget the American Civil War of 1860 that was fought between the Northern part of the Nation, and the Southern part, when the country itself split practically down the middle into the Union and the Confederacy? Forgetting all the romanticism of war, the Civil War was fought for more than one reason. Some revolving around the culture of slavery that was prevalent at the time in the southern states, some of it for political reasons behind Abraham Lincoln becoming President, and some revolving around the growing power of the Federal government over the States that some felt was becoming an issue.

Let's also not forget the two World Wars of the 20th century. The First World War, the United States, entered into late, within the last year or so of the fighting avoiding the majority of the fighting that had erupted. But the reasons were no different than any other engagements that the nation found itself in, by deciding to back up US allies in the face of an oppressive enemy that would have stopped at nothing short of total decimation.

No one will forget the Second World War (WWII) that was fought between the Allied powers, and the Axis powers, nor the bombing of Pearl Harbor by the Japanese that finally broke American isolationism and declared war on both Germany and Japan. This incensed the entire nation into entering a war that before 1941 was viewed as "A European problem."

In fact, it was the supreme catalyst in the 1940's that transformed America from a republic into a super power. It demonstrated American ingenuity when the entire country and its citizens changed its economy and became an industrial powerhouse. Even to this day, this still impacts the United States as one of the most forward superpowers.

This all demonstrates that while War itself is horrible and ghastly, in a lot of ways it's still an unavoidable situation that forces everyone to take up arms against others, and nothing is proven greater in the US history. Whether it was for Independence, to fight off a fascist regime and protect our allies, or fight against others over political differences, or against genocide, land-grabbing as we've seen in the expansion wars that went westward, wars have been fought for a myriad of reasons.

However a change in the United States' demeanor changed after World War II, and it wasn't evident until the Vietnam War in the 1960's that this change came over America and how it fought its wars.

As most people know, after World War II, there emerged two super powers, the United States, and the Soviet Union. Realistically, both were dynamically opposed to each other's ideology. The United States represented Democracy and Capitalism while the Soviet Union instead represented Communism (or, a form of it) and chose to combine both state and economy together.

Vietnam was at war with itself in the North and South, much like the US was a century earlier. The South was backed by Democracy, and the North falling to Communism. Of course, US couldn't let communism win, and joined in to back up the South. As most people know, the US lost that war during the fall of Saigon, and since then most wars have been fought for only one reason: Corporate Greed, and nothing more.

Greed in Military Corporations is really no secret. War makes money for the RIGHT people (Republicans), for they are set to make the most profits from it. While historically there are arms dealers, weapons manufacturers and wholesalers, private security firms, and contractors who build things for a living, never before at any point in history, has war been fought solely for Corporate gain. That's the problem with corporations instigating wars to generate profits.

Look to some examples that have been cropped up within the last 30 years. The US during the 80's sold its military surplus weaponry to foreign powers, such as "Freedom Fighters" in Afghanistan, arming Saddam Hussein when he rose to power, Saudi and Syrian soldiers, and more, for the sole reason to fight against the Soviets.

Once the Soviet Union collapsed in the early 1990's, those weapons were then turned against the US. Saddam Hussein invaded Kuwait in the first Gulf War, and we backed Kuwait by going in and fighting Saddam there.

However, part of the deal that had been struck was that American and Western-backed Corporations would go in and be granted access to the oil fields, and to take back weapons that were sold to those fighting not even 10 years before. That plus building contractors would come in and charge money for rebuilding Kuwait and surrounding nations. Most of them also were corporate-backed with almost none of the money going to local businesses that knew the area.

In fact, looking at the wars that are now being fought in the Middle East that began a little over 10 years after the first Gulf War, and after the invasion of Afghanistan, President George Bush Jr. turned American weapons on Iraq and threatened to attack Iraq. He threatened to oust Saddam Hussein once and for all, all as revenge for the 9/11 attacks that happened two years earlier.

WTF? Despite the overwhelming evidence that Iraq had nothing to do with the terrorist attacks two years earlier, and even more evident was that Hussein didn't have weaponry stockpiled, and an overwhelming opposition to the war itself, the United States and NATO members attacked Iraq's borders in March of 2003. That lie which has proven to be politically and private corporation (military and construction corporations) backed – is still defended by the Republicans seeking presidential office in 2016. *Can you believe that shit? – the editor.*

As demonstrated by the first Gulf War, various corporations carved up Iraq's landscape, like a turkey, among themselves. The most famous corporation being Haliburton (VP Dick Cheney's partner- in-crime). Cheney still on their payroll (a violation of US law), he owned stocks and bonds and other investments with Halliburton (another violation of US law), and they came in to "safeguard" the oil reserves, vowing to use it for what was right for the people. Unfortunately, it wasn't right for Iraqi benefit, it was for Republican corporate owner benefit.

That's even not to mention the other corporations who came in to make money off of the War from construction contractors, electricity providers, mercenaries and private security firms (most famous of which was "Blackwater.") and many others.

All of this build up to a huge problem and has given rise to the Military Industrial Complex that has sprung up to rule all aspects of American economics and politics. While the Military Industrial Complex (MIC) isn't a place, it is a machine that fuels war, for profit, that has grown to take over all sensibility since Vietnam.

In fact, it's become such a fixation on American Politics growing to the point that Military industries take up more than half of the United States annual budget, with most of that money going to corporations for military weaponry and research.

The United States Government doesn't make weapons but instead outsources it all to Corporations, some of which are even foreign. Tanks, Planes, Guns, Ammo, Kevlar Vests, Automobiles, Trucks, and food rations all come from corporations that produce these goods. The boots soldiers wear, their clothing, even the steel used to fashion the weapons all come from corporations that fuel the Military Industry. All of this for the sake of peace and the American way. *Yeah – right! – Bullshit, the editor.*

How deeply embedded are the Corporations in American Politics? *They are so deeply embedded in the pockets of American Congressmen, that the Congressmen can feel them when they scratch their balls – the editor.* Take as an example, years ago, a bill was going through Congress to save $100 million a year by discontinuing funding of an obsolete Jet Engine, that's rarely seen any combat recently. There ended up being an uproar, with one Congressman accusing the one who wrote the bill of being a traitor, and that the jets were needed to keep America safe. Besides, the jobs that it created benefited the economy.

Of course, no one had thought to mention that this Congressman, who accused the other of being a traitor, was on the payroll of the Corporation that made these jets, with stock options, but the damage was done. The bill did not pass and was set aside. Even today, those Jets are being built, but not being used. Instead, Congress decided to save money by cutting social programs for the poor, the sick, and the crippled.

There's no stopping them either, not as long as the American people sit back and let it happen. Only time will tell if anyone ever decides to do anything about it. To give another idea, billions of dollars is being poured into building weaponry that isn't being used. In other words, they are developing impractical weaponry. Billions more are being maintained to store and house tools that are old and obsolete that will never see use anymore.

All of this is going on while people die because they can't afford healthcare insurance. People go hungry because they don't get paid enough at work to eat and get their children enough nutrients.

The land of the free, and home of the brave indeed. While the citizens continually fall to the wayside in the name of military profiteering, at least the US is well-armed, well-stocked, and ready to march to war in order to line the pockets of those whose only true goal is the greedy accumulation of wealth and mass murder in the name of profiteering. *– Yeah, the RIGHT people. – the editor*

CHAPTER V

A Bullet to the Brain of a Corrupt System

Part 1: Ethics and how it applies towards our Government

Morality. Virtue. Honesty. Integrity. All of those words are synonyms of the word "Ethics", which according to Webster's Dictionary, is defined as "the body of moral principles or values governing, or distinctive of a particular culture or group." Or, "a complex of moral precepts held or rules of conduct followed by an individual." In etymological terms, the word Ethics originated from the Greek word ēthikós, which is a compilation of the words "ethos" and "ikos." That essentially meant, during the time of the Greeks, that Ethics was the system of governing morality among the Greek culture, and how people should conduct themselves in regards to their respective societies, and for the state itself.

However, like most words throughout history, the meaning of words have changed, and different cultures have come and gone, changed or adapted, disappeared and came back around once more. In the modern sense, as the Webster's Dictionary definition has shown, Ethics is a guide for morality and the rules that self-govern a person in how they wish to conduct themselves. Having good ethics is tantamount to functioning well in society, and the ethics that our current American culture values, above all else, is a willingness to work with other people, and to value personal freedoms, and basic human rights above all else, while maintaining a level of respect for one another.

Today, having good Ethics basically means that the individual puts others over their own selfish desires and builds up those around him, in his community and abroad, instead of tearing them down for their own personal gain.

A good example of this comes from a Boston Ethics experiment, conducted in the early 70's by an elementary school teacher named Jane Elliott. Jane did this shortly after the assassination of Martin Luther King Jr. She formed an exercise that she used to experiment on her third grade classroom that's been dubbed "The Blue Eyes - Brown eyes experiment." The experiment was pretty simple in design, in all honesty. She simply separated her classroom into two distinct groups. One group led by the "blue eyes" where every student who had blue eyes belonged to it and the secondary group was led by the "brown eyes", where each student who had brown eyes was a part of that one.

The experiment started off simple enough. One group was at first treated better than the other group, such as the blue eyes in the class being allowed extra time at recess, first pick of the toys, allowed to associate with anyone they wished (as long as they were only a part of their particular group), and so on. Plus, they had received lenient punishment if they did wrong, as opposed to the brown-eyed group who often received arbitrary punishment for even the smallest infractions, and were given unfair disadvantages or punishments and spoken off negatively.

Not surprising to all, the blue eyed group internalized the roles better and acted superior to their brown eyed counterpart.

However, when the roles became reversed, and the Brown eyes took over as the dominant role, a surprising twist happened. The Brown eyes had already experienced the worst, unfair disadvantages that the blue eyes had had against them. Instead, realizing that they were now dominant and were allowed to abuse the blue eyes, surprisingly showed mercy, humanity and ethics with the blue eyes, and they started to help them instead of being a an unethical group.

While Jane Elliott's lessons were more in line with teaching how not to be racist through shared ignorance, the lessons that the experiment showcases and reverberates far more than one issue of American Culture. In fact, the students themselves after the experiment had gone live had been monitored throughout their school careers, reuniting with their teacher 15 years later, and showing the kind of adults that they had become. The majority of them showing high levels of Ethics, and morality, who were willing to help others, and become model citizens themselves in regards to helping people out. Not only did they show that they could be Ethical, but they could do it and still be successful.

Most people, though, will look at that and wonder how it correlates with Politicians, and what this can for with politics and politicians right now. Unlike the school children who took well to the lessons they were given, most Politicians today seem to have no issues whatsoever with being unethical in their mannerism. Today, Congress has an approval rating of 14%, while the President of the United States, Barack Obama, has an approval rating of 45%. Even the Supreme Court isn't immune to criticism from the American public at a rating of only 48%. That shows that more than half of American citizens do not trust any of the branches of our government and believe fully that none of the politicians who work in our government are doing a good job.

This is because of the endless negativity that surrounds the world of politics, giving it a seemingly negative atmosphere of the "me, me, me, me" culture of excess narcissism and how no one seems interested in working together, even among members of their own party. Because of this, Politicians end up focusing on themselves more than anything else, often forgetting the constituents in their respective districts who voted for them in the first place.

They forget that their job isn't to be all about them and their crazy wants and needs and their constant chance at being the top dog on Capitol Hill, but instead to represent the people – their constituents. In fact, more often than not they often forget that Democracy is not about getting everything that they want. But, is supposed to be a system of government that survives through compromise, and by coming to an understanding with one another to achieve a goal, by listening to all sides of the debate and working for what's best for the people, not the politician is key to being a good and ethical politician.

After all, if it's all about them, how is that Ethical in any way? – the editor.

Quick answer: It's not. It's selfish, and only perpetuates the culture of selfishness that permeates Washington D.C. The Politicians forget about the people that they were sworn to protect, and represent, and uphold the values that we, of the United States, hold dear. These include the constitution, but instead they choose to take advantage when fighting among one another. Instead, we should take lessons from the Boston Experiment, and perform something on a big bigger scale that Jane Elliott had initiated with her students, except of course perform it on older people instead who should, for the most part, know better.

Each new politician who enters into the field, and who has never governed before on a federal scale should be given a test that's similar in design to the Blue eyes-Brown Eyes one. Instead, however, they should also be given a test in Ethics as well, and re-taught ethics and morality. First off, with the test, it should be treated like any sort of evaluation, where they're given a sort of psych evaluation to determine if they're even capable of morality, before simply being passed off to the next part.

Naturally, if they fail to pass that portion, they should not be sworn into office. However, if they do, and they're given the approval to continue on, then they should be given a written test, followed by the experiment where they're treated as second class citizens among the other junior electives before the roles are reversed, and so on.

And, like the students of the Boston experiment, they should also be continually monitored throughout their careers to see if they continue to adhere to the guidelines of Ethics that the experiment is created to uphold.

After following an initial trial period which should not last longer than is needed, perhaps a few months, then they're allowed to perform their civic duties as elected representatives. In fact, all elected officials within the government should be overseen on this sort of system, from the Judicial, Executive, and Legislative branch, by a group of non-partisan members that do not work for the government, but for the people, so as to bypass any sort of bias along party lines.

Violations of the Ethics agreement should be dealt with heavily as well. After all, we elected these officials into a powerful capacity. We voted them in to help create laws, to help with the yearly budget for the American people, to be our President, as well as vetted to serve us on the Supreme Court. We should hold these people to a higher standards than most others within our country, and they should not be allowed to let us down. Penalties for them should be very heavy, and ultimately, if we're to trust them with improving our way of life, and being the vanguards of our culture, Ethics, and Morality they must prove themselves. *Some of the most lenient penalties for small infractions should include heavy fines and lashes with a wet noodle – the editor.*

After all, if they take bribes, or are found profiting off of another's misery either through national disasters, or through war, or through any other means that they should not be … to keep them non-biased, we should hit them where they'll hurt the most – A Bullet to the Brain. Small offenses by fining them all the money they've stolen and taking away their salary and perks and their jobs. And, and for severe repeated violations – A Bullet to the Brain. Simple.

The money harvested in small offense restitution could be put into the economy to pay for services that are much needed such as infrastructure repair, schools, hospitals, police, and fire services.

If they continue to violate the law and circumvent it for their own selfish gain – the bullet does the job. *Show no mercy. – the editor.*

There is no reason as to why a governing system should be allowed to circumvent the law and get away with wrong-doing. In fact, too often, right now, politicians use the clout of their subordinates, and the murkiness of the law to their advantage to keep their crimes hidden from the public, and they should not be allowed to do so.

We could also use the non-partisan group to find those who had previously been fined or Politicians who have been caught doing something unethical, they should immediately be impeached, and all rights and entitlements that they have earned revoked and put back into the budget for social issues.

Pensions should only cover those politicians who have served with Ethics and pride, and should not be given to those who have essentially been "fired" from their position for Ethics reasons.

Should the law have been broken while under the Politicians care, and all evidence leads back to them - bullet time, no questions asked.

How often has a politician been caught with bribe money in their pocket, or have taken money from a lobbyist to buy votes, or been caught in a fraudulent situation? More often than you'd think, which has led to the decline of faith of the American public in Congress. Once laws have been broken, instead of a lengthy court date, and the court dates being moved further to the point of becoming moot, the offending party should simply be led to the room where the bullet will be implanted with force. This is to insure that any politician who chooses to break the law will realize they cannot hide behind it to have their crime pushed back till enough time has passed for the American Public to forget about it.

If all of these suggestions are implemented, there is no doubt that the quality of the United States of America will improve drastically. Instead of starting to lag behind educationally, fiscally, economically, and all, we'd see efforts from our elected officials to improve our way of life, with our view on Ethics guiding us to improve our human rights for all people, and not just themselves.

Not only will we have a government that works for the people, and can restore trust in our Representatives, but we'll enjoy greater freedoms, with less government being about only ripping off the taxpayers.

Not only that but the stiff penalties that any politician will face if they deviate from the law will deter anyone from working outside of the boundary that the American people themselves set for the Politicians.

And in the end, isn't that what we all want? To improve our way of life, and see to it that we aren't just a resource for greed for those in power. Rather than having the pains of a revolution reset the clock, we won't need one if we keep a close eye on Congress and all elected officials.

Final Thoughts

this is your world. shape it or someone else will.

That all is basically the end of this series. I have covered only a few of the major issues facing the US and there are many, many more.

As we've seen throughout the various chapters, there are a lot of problems that plague the United States currently in these times and I've just touched on them. Don't think these are problems that only the people of this current generation has faced, however. There have always been problems that the country has faced in the past since its inception.

Even within the first year of the founding of this Nation there were problems, all the way through the 1800's, through the 1900's, and into the new millennium. However, the difference back in the past was that the problems were solved through grit, determination, and the power of the vote, as well as the power of people who gathered en masse to change society and its laws. We've seen it before, and we'll more than likely see it again, but only if we want to bring back that power to the citizens.

The citizenry needs to first wake up, though, as we've seen in the first chapter of this book. With the power of Propaganda and Partisanship, we've divided the citizens of this nation into two separate camps and pitted them against each other as members of the Government profit off of it.

With two parties, Republican and Democrats, we've divided into blue vs. red, liberal vs. conservative, and have fought against our own economic interests for the sake of hurting or winning against the opposing side. They've even utilized Fox News to drum up their major support for one side, which has fueled the plethora of Republican Candidates in this election cycle to harm everyone with their choice of actions to enact. Truly, this was the best that could be offered to us from one side of the aisle.

As we saw in Chapter Two regarding foreign policies, the tactics of the Republican Party just don't work at all as well, though the Democrats don't get off Scott-free either. Previous President George W. Bush and Vice President Dick Cheney set the tone for the new millennium, regarding politics and political choices and also profiteering off the lies. Yes, it was their choices and policies that led to the current predicament that we now face especially with the growth of ISIS, et al., international terrorism. They are responsible for how we treat foreign enemy combatants with torture, and with citizens with the loss of social benefits.

It's also indicative of how the international community views us in light of our actions, especially since we've started the wars for profiteering while we're fighting with NATO allies in the Middle East.

Chapter Three, of course, discusses how it's not just a problem internationally for us, but a problem we also have to deal with at home because of domestic terrorism, and the fact that it comes from various unlikely sources as well.

For starters, we've got the problem of the Police, and how slowly they're becoming more and more aggressive thanks to anti-terrorism measures that were designed to be a rapid response to terrorist actions. Instead, these actions have been turned on the citizens, and the growing fatalities that we've seen from Police acting as terrorists are making us not trust the police any longer.

From there, we've lost the war on drugs that have been a staple of 90's propaganda, such as D.A.R.E and other programs but have correlation effects that led to the rise of prison sentences and an increase of the prisoner population and profiteering off of it. *And this is just from smoking a doobie. – the editor.*

How did this all come about you might ask yourself? Simply put, the Government can't keep paying for the things it needs to be, like all civilized countries, social welfare and assistance programs. Because of that, we've allowed corporations to come in, take over private functions of the country and allowed them carte blanche access to dictate prices, services, and how we as Americans have access to those things such as basic infrastructure, Firemen, Police, health insurance, and other necessities.

As has been proven time and time again in this book, and has been mentioned in every possible part that can be said, there needs to be change. There needs to be a call to action. There needs to be an uproar of United States citizens that can jump start a second wave of revolution to get back our country once and for all, back on the right track.

In fact, there needs to be a massive wake-up call that takes all of us Americans out of an apathetic and drunken or drug-induced (pharmaceutical or illegal drug) stupor and forces us to realize the problems that we've allowed ourselves to get stuck into.

Not only that, but we need to take responsibility for what we've allowed to occur and finally fix the problem. We need to go out, we need to vote, we need to vote, we need to vote. We need to take out the corrupt police, the corrupt politicians, the corrupt CEO's, the Fat cats of Wall Street and return to a simpler time that was good for everyone, for every race, of every religion, and every sexuality. *We need to allow women's rights. -the editor.*

We need to finally re-learn to stand up for ourselves as Americans.

And if we don't?

We'll simply fall to the wayside of history, as every other empire before us. This country will fall, and without action it will fall hard from grace. History has proven that it is not kind to fallen Empires. After all, there's no longer a Roman Empire, a Holy Roman Empire, no Ottoman Empire, no Austrian-Hungarian Empire, no Soviet Union, no major empire. Even England, itself, is a shadow of its former glory. We, too, will be a part of that failure as we see our freedoms slowly being chipped away. We will become a land of prisoners and inmates, fearing for our very lives as psychopaths with badges roam the street, and the corrupt and unethical start wars outside and inside the USA and become rich off of our backs. We'll become slaves to the very ideals we use to enjoy and strive for.

However, as has been proven by this entire book.

All it takes, if it comes down to it,

Is a Bullet to the Brain!

www.ingramcontent.com/pod-product-compliance
Lightning Source LLC
Chambersburg PA
CBHW071201280526
45787CB00002B/565